THE SOCIETY OF ILLUSTRATORS
TWENTY FIFTH ANNUAL OF
AMERICAN ILLUSTRATION
ILLUSTRATORS
25

EXHIBITION HELD IN THE GALLERIES OF THE SOCIETY OF ILLUSTRATORS
MUSEUM OF AMERICAN ILLUSTRATION, 128 EAST 63RD STREET, NEW YORK
FEBRUARY 2-APRIL 13, 1983

SOCIETY OF ILLUSTRATORS, INC.
128 EAST 63RD STREET, NEW YORK, N.Y. 10021

ISBN-0-942604-02-4
Library of Congress Catalog Card Number 59-10849

Printed and bound in Tokyo, Japan by Dai Nippon Printing Co. Ltd. through
DNP (America), Inc.

Typography: Advani Typographic Associates, New York City

Distributors to the trade in the United States:
Robert Silver Associates: 95 Madison Avenue, New York, N.Y. 10016

Distributors to the trade in Canada:
General Publishing Co. Ltd., 30 Lesmill Road, Don Mills, Ontario, Canada M3B 2T6

Distributed in Contintental Europe by:
Feffer and Simons, B.V., 170 Rijnkade, Weesp, Netherlands

Distributed throughout the rest of the world by:
Fleetbooks, S.A., c/o Feffer and Simons, Inc., 100 Park Avenue, New York, N.Y. 10017

Publisher: Madison Square Press Inc., 10 East 23rd Street, New York City, N.Y. 10010

Robert Anthony, Designer   Charles Kreloff, Assistant Designer   Art Weithas, Editor

THE SOCIETY OF ILLUSTRATORS
TWENTY FIFTH ANNUAL OF
AMERICAN ILLUSTRATION
ILLUSTRATORS
25

1/25 PUBLISHED FOR THE SOCIETY OF ILLUSTRATORS BY MADISON SQUARE PRESS, INC., NEW YORK 10010
DISTRIBUTED BY ROBERT SILVER ASSOCIATES, NEW YORK 10016

President's Message

This Twenty-Fifth Annual of American Illustration represents a significant publishing achievement. For the first time, all the reproductions appear in the original colors of their creation. This added dimension should be of real value for students, professional artists and those who commission this art form.

The impact and emotion of color should also extend the vision of the insightful historian. Each day, week and month, in all forms of media, illustrators portray current ideas, personalities and events.

There is a meaning in these images beyond their techniques and a collective content that reveals much about our culture and the world during the past year.

The Society of Illustrators is now proud to bring it all to you—in full living color!

JOHN WITT

Illustration: Burt Silverman

Two and a half decades.
A Silver Anniversary.

This book is the twenty fifth annual published by the Society of Illustrators. During those 25 years America has experienced dramatic, emotional, social, economic and scientific changes.

Who shall ever forget the shock and anguish of President Kennedy's assassination? The spiritual turmoil of the civil rights movement? The sense of guilt and frustration of participation in the Vietnam war or our pride and exhilaration in placing the American flag on the moon?

During these years, the illustrator graphically chronicled events as they occurred. Many were reproduced in the annual as some of the best illustrations of that year.

Norman Rockwell's painting of two burly government agents escorting a black child in pigtails to school was a magnificent example of pictorial editorialism. Austin Briggs' and John Groths' drawings of the Vietnam conflict were superb, and again Rockwell's painting of the moon landing caught the very awesome quality of the event. Fred Otnes' assemblage of the civil rights movement was graphic journalism at its best.

The same years witnessed many changes in the field of illustration as well.

By 1959 the glamour years of illustration had passed. The reading public was diminishing. The Saturday Evening Post was yielding to Life and Look. Magazines were folding. The role of the illustrator as a means of enticing readership was dwindling. TV was insistently and ever increasingly invading the home.

The Art Directors annual, which had provided the showplace for the illustrator in the past, now devoted a minimum of pages to illustration with most of its pages given to photography and TV.

To meet the challenge, illustration was changing. It was becoming more colorful, more design conscious, more demanding of attention.

It was in this grim atmosphere that the Society of Illustrators bravely decided to hold an exhibition of the best illustrations of the previous year and to reproduce them in its own annual.

Overcoming monumental obstacles, the exhibition opened January 15, 1959.

Its success was instant. To quote David Stone, the first exhibition committee chairman: "For a solid month capacity crowds enjoyed the show. Illustrators seemed reassured, buyers were impressed and students were inspired by the highly professional and varied display. New talents and trends were recognized while more traditional values were also represented. Every serious effort in illustration was covered".

"We are confident that we have brought about an inspirational force for illustration that will grow in quality and importance in the years to come".

A very prophetic comment. Over the years the annual has stayed true to its premise of presenting the best contemporary illustration and in the process it has recorded a changing America.

Art Weithas

FRED OTNES *Illustrators 14, 1972*

BERNIE FUCHS *Illustrators '65*

ROCKWELL *Illustrators '66-'67*

ROBERT GUZZI *Illustrators 14, 1972*

JOHN GROTH *U.S. Marine Corps. Combat Art Collection*

AUSTIN BRIGGS *Illustrators 11, 1969*

NORMAN ROCKWELL *Illustrators 13, 1971*

ROBERT WEAVER *Illustrators '64*

GILBERT L. STONE *Illustrators XII, 1970*

BERNIE FUCHS *Illustrators '66-'67*

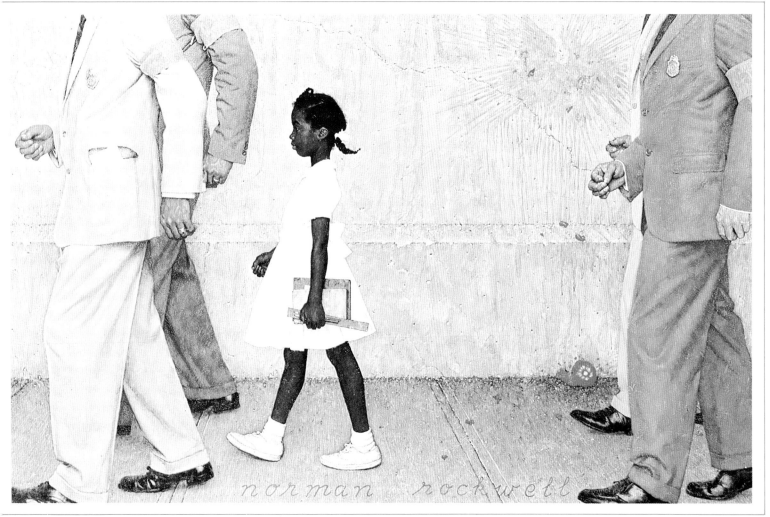

NORMAN ROCKWELL *Illustrators '64*

Hall of Fame Award

As the name implies, the Hall of Fame awards are presented by the Society of Illustrators each year to those artists who have made an outstanding contribution to the art of illustration.

The list is long and impressive and the recipients are the greatest illustrators of the past and present. The first award was made to Norman Rockwell in 1958.

This year's award winners are Mark English, the sensitive, innovative painter; Franklin Booth, the extraordinary line artist and Noel Sickles, the versatile and highly respected illustrator. The last two awards were presented posthumously.

Hall of Fame Chairman: Willis Pyle

Hall of Fame Committee:
Past Presidents of the Society
Walter Brooks
Harry Carter
Stevan Dohanos
Tran Mawicke
Charles McVicker
John A. Moodie
Howard Munce
Alvin J. Pimsler
Warren Rogers
William Schneider
Shannon Stirnweis
David K. Stone

1 Norman Rockwell 1958
2 Dean Cornwell 1959
3 Harold von Schmidt 1959
4 Fred Cooper 1960
5 Floyd Davis 1961
6 Edward Wilson 1962
7 Walter Biggs 1963
8 Arthur William Brown 1964
9 Al Parker 1965
10 Al Dorne 1966
11 Robert Fawcett 1967
12 Peter Helck 1968
13 Austin Briggs 1969
14 Rube Goldberg 1970
15 Stevan Dohanos 1971
16 Ray Prohaska 1972
17 Jon Whitcomb 1973
18 Tom Lovell 1974
19 Charles Dana Gibson* 1974
20 N.C. Wyeth* 1974
21 Bernie Fuchs 1975
22 Maxfield Parrish* 1975
23 Howard Pyle* 1975
24 John Falter 1976
25 Winslow Homer* 1976
26 Harvey Dunn* 1976
27 Robert Peak 1977
28 Wallace Morgan* 1977
29 J.C. Leyendecker* 1977
30 Coby Whitmore 1978
31 Norman Price* 1978
32 Frederic Remington* 1978
33 Ben Stahl 1979
34 Edwin Austin Abbey* 1979
35 Lorraine Fox* 1979
36 Saul Tepper 1980
37 Howard Chandler Christy* 1980
38 James Montgomery Flagg* 1980
39 Stan Galli 1981
40 Frederic R. Gruger* 1981
41 John Gannam* 1981
42 John Clymer 1982
43 Henry P. Raleigh* 1982
44 Eric (Carl Erickson)* 1982

presented posthumously

Hall of Fame 1983

MARK ENGLISH (b. 1933)
Interviewed by Anna Lee Fuchs

Anna Lee Fuchs: Is it true you've received more medals from the Society of Illustrators than any other illustrator?

Mark English: When the Twenty Years of Award Winners book came out I received a letter from the Society stating that I had received more awards in the Society's Annual exhibitions than any other illustrator.

ALF: How many years have you been in the illustration business?

ME: Twenty-one years.

ALF: And before that what did you do?

ME: Well . . . my first job was picking cotton in Texas. I got out of the cotton fields by learning to paint signs. I chased rodeos, painting "Welcome Rodeo Fans" signs on store windows. My first big job was painting billboards for an outdoor sign company. Then I was drafted into the Army where I painted signs again—for the Training Aid Section.

ALF: I heard once you painted signs on the latrines?

ME: That was part of my Army assignment.

ALF: From there, where did you go?

ME: There was no place to go but up. I was stationed in El Paso, where I met Harvey Schmidt, who had just graduated from the University of Texas, and was on his way to New York with Robert Benton, who later became the art director for Esquire. They recommended that I go to Art Center in Los Angeles, which I did when I got out of the Army.

ALF: Did you draw pictures when you were little?

ME: Yeah, I did. John Collier and I talked about that recently over lunch. We were being interviewed by a Japanese writer who said he noticed that an awful lot of illustrators came from Texas and he'd wondered why. We didn't have a good answer for that except that there wasn't much to do in Texas except draw pictures. From the time I can remember, all my brothers and I sat around and drew pictures on rainy days.

ALF: After you left Art Center what was your first job?

ME: Art Director on an automobile account for N.W. Ayer Advertising Agency in Detroit.

ALF: Did you do any work as an art director?

ME: Not finished art work. I did fancy layouts, the kind that make illustrators nervous, but I was only using photographers

at the time, not illustrators.

ALF: Did that experience help you when you became an illustrator?

ME: Yes, I think it did. I became more understanding of the art director's problems.

ALF: What was your biggest break in becoming a nationally known illustrator? And is there one job that had a great effect on your career?

ME: Yes, there was one job. I had moved to Connecticut and in my first year there I made about 20% of the salary that I had made in my last year in Detroit. It was a tough year and I had a lot of time on my hands. I think not having much work maybe enhanced my career more than anything else. I spent a lot of time experimenting, trying to come up with something unique and different, and I think towards the end of that year I managed to do that on a job for Readers' Digest.

ALF: Was that the "Little Women" series?

ME: Yes, and I think 3 or 4 of the illustrations were accepted into the Society's Annual Exhibition that year. One of them won an award and got me a little attention. After that I got into magazines and my career was launched.

ALF: Do you still illustrate for magazines?

ME: No, not very much. Most of my magazine career ended 6 or 7 years ago.

ALF: Why are you in Kansas?

ME: Hallmark asked me to come out here to teach for a year, so I took a year off and taught classes 2 hours a day. I've been comfortable here so I've stayed.

ALF: Do you ever want to go back to Texas?

ME: I have dreams of that now and then, but I just bought a farm in Missouri, so I guess I'll be living and working there.

ALF: How do you feel about competing for the same jobs with your close illustrator friends?

ME: I began with an agent, Tom Holloway, who also represented Bernie Fuchs and Austin Briggs. They were established and hot in New York while I was a newcomer, inexperienced and very unsure of myself. It was tough competition and a strange way of getting started. But I managed to get going in spite of it. I think the association was good for me. After a while I really never felt any head-on kind of competition; in most cases the client wanted either Bernie or Austin or they wanted me.

ALF: Since you're one of the most copied illustrators in the country would you comment on whether you think style is more important than technique?

ME: Absolutely! The words technique and style are often confused. Bernie's technique or my technique may be copied, but the style is something that cannot be imitated. That's what separates us from the copiers.

ALF: Do you find that students ask about technique first?

ME: Yes, they do. I understand that, though. I was very anxious to learn technique. I thought it was the solution to all problems. I found out later that it wasn't. Technique is not really important. Your point of view is the thing that comes through. And today Bernie has changed his technique, I've changed mine, Bob Heindel has changed his and we're still recognizable.

ALF: Do you usually work in the same medium?

ME: I learned to paint with acrylics. If you can learn to paint with acrylics you can handle anything. But I couldn't go back to it now. About 7 or 8 years ago I started using oils and oil crayons and the combination of the two is the medium I'm most comfortable with now.

ALF: Is it true that the Illustrators Workshop was started because of you and your desire to teach?

ME: The Illustrators Workshop happened because Art Center invited me to take a few years off to teach in L.A. I didn't feel that I could do that. I suggested that they send a few people back East and I would try to put together a group that would teach a workshop. They did and I did and that's how it happened.

ALF: Would you rather teach professionals or students who haven't been in the job market yet?

ME: That's a tough question. To generalize, the easiest time for me was when I was teaching at Hallmark. There were a great many talented people in my classes and it was rewarding to teach those who were so interested and competent.

ALF: I understand that your son is also an illustrator? Is he very good?

ME: Yes, speaking without prejudice, he's very good. He's one of the best young illustrators I've seen in a long time.

ALF: What's his name?

ME: His name is Mark Littlejohn English but he prefers to use the name John.

ALF: How would you define an illustrator?

ME: There are all kinds of illustrators, but a good illustrator is an artist. He makes pictures on assignment, on commissions; he solves other people's problems pictorially. I think that pretty well describes it.

ALF: Do you find it interesting to work as an artist for a gallery?

ME: Yes, but sometimes I find it discouraging. The thing I like about the illustration business as opposed to the gallery business is that in illustration the good guys generally win, which is not always true in the gallery business. There are very successful, not very competent painters and very unsuccessful, competent painters out there— more so than in the illustration business. I do gallery paintings because I enjoy pursuing a train of thought through a series of paintings, or simply doing a painting for myself, hopefully selling it or showing it in a gallery. But I do like illustration, too.

Hall of Fame 1983

NOEL SICKLES 1910-1982

He grew up in Chillicothe, Ohio. His father was a railroad man who drew intricate, loving and naive pictures of his railroad memories. Noel Sickles' formal art education came from the Landon School of Art, a correspondence course in cartooning. His informal art education came from the study of illustrations found in the books and publications at the libraries he haunted. He once told me that Charles Keene (1823-1891), the English cartoonist, and Alfred Sisley (1839-1899), the Paris-born English impressionist, were his great influences.

At 19, he was a full-time political cartoonist for the *Ohio State Journal.* Three years later he began a cartoon strip which became a challenge to that art forever after. *Scorchy Smith* still remains the ultimate model for the adventure strip cartoonist.

When I first met Noel in 1940, he had abandoned cartooning to begin his career in free-lance illustration and the work he was producing was, to my young eyes, nothing short of magical. The ease with which he drew and the scope and variety of his abilities were awesome. As the inevitability of WWII became obvious, Noel's knowledge of military hardware led to commissions from *Life* to acquaint its readership with the events to which the camera was not privy. At the time, he had married his beloved Louise and had left New York City for Valley Cottage in Rockland County, N.Y., not far from his old and close friend, Milt Caniff. My wife, Wende, and I rented a house nearby and it was from there that I left for Washington, D.C. A year later, I recommended Noel as a civilian employee in our group, the Identification and Characteristic Section of Navy Intelligence. For almost three years, we shared a studio close to the Lincoln Memorial. In those years, Noel produced some of his finest works. The illustrations for Newsmap, a joint Army-Navy venture, were adventuresome and bold, enormously detailed and drawn without human models and under impossible deadlines. For Dr. Howard Rome of the Navy's Neuro-Psychiatric Section, Noel drew highly sensitive works in a style that would come to full fruition in his revolutionary "Old Man and the Sea" illustrations. Until Hank Ketchum arrived, Noel did most of the cartooning as well.

Near the end of the war, Si Coleman, our tough and brilliant art director, laid out what was to be the last Navy Day poster. Noel painted it. That poster is noteworthy because Edward Steichen, the great Navy photographer, had ideas of his own for the project. When presented with Noel's painting, Capt. Steichen, a wonderful and gifted painter, cheerfully admitted that there was no contest.

Full recognition came to Noel following the war years. At one point the *Saturday Evening Post* offered him a carte blanche arrangement in which he could chose from any manuscript he might find appealing. Now his work appeared in all the major illustrated magazines and in many of the books published by *Reader's Digest.* The quality of the work was superb. Never content with his output, Noel destroyed many illustrations that would have elated art editors and left most of his contemporaries thoroughly envious.

And of course, he attracted many imitators. The style however, was dependent on a remarkable sense of drawing that was the undoing of so many of his photo-oriented followers. Noel's illustrations could involve 70 figures, horses, wagons and rugged landscapes. Each face in the figure described a personality and the costumes were not only individual, but accurate.

Noel continued his assignments for *Life.* Some were done with brush (he chewed the tips and used the frayed and tattered ends to indicate shrubbery, grasses, etc.), India ink and charcoal. The color illustrations were done with colored India inks until the value of his work was fully understood and he changed to the more permanent media.

Life sponsored an exhibition of his work that toured the world. In Cairo, Egypt, the exhibition was stolen and the originals to "The Seige of Leningrad", Hemingway's "The Old Man and the Sea", the WWII Trials and many others were lost forever. Happily some of his best works are in the collections of the *National Geographic* and *Reader's Digest.*

In his last years, Noel devoted himself to an old love—the depiction of the West. His *Saturday Evening Post* illustrations of the West were of such excellence and created such interest that he was encouraged to continue in that genre. The paintings that followed have a verity that has escaped many of the recent painters of the West. They are infused with history and are unrelenting in the recapturing of the space and light and the vastness of the early West.

Noel had no hobbies—there was no golf or tennis. He had two loves—Louise and his work. He worked constantly, researching and ever improving that miraculous ability to draw. In his moments of relaxation, he was a charming companion. Bob Blattner of *Reader's Digest* told me that he never knew anyone to enjoy humor as much as Noel. He was a good and loyal friend, always willing to share a new enthusiasm or discovery.

In his Christmas Day, 1982 Steve Canyon strip, Milt Caniff wrote: "This restless genius was the greatest natural cartoonist I ever knew. Now he is dead! All that talent still unused and every cartoonist feels cheated of what might yet have come from his magic hand." Noel is gone and the wonderful work he produced is scattered. He was a cartoonist, an illustrator and a painter. He was an exemplar, a mentor and a giant who now takes his place with those rare few greats whose names appear in the Society of Illustrators Hall of Fame.

Harry Devlin

David Lewis writing in his log by Noel Sickles
Courtesy ©National Geographic Society

Illustrations by Noel Sickles "The Old Man and the Sea" by Ernest Hemingway
Donated by Mrs. Noel Sickles

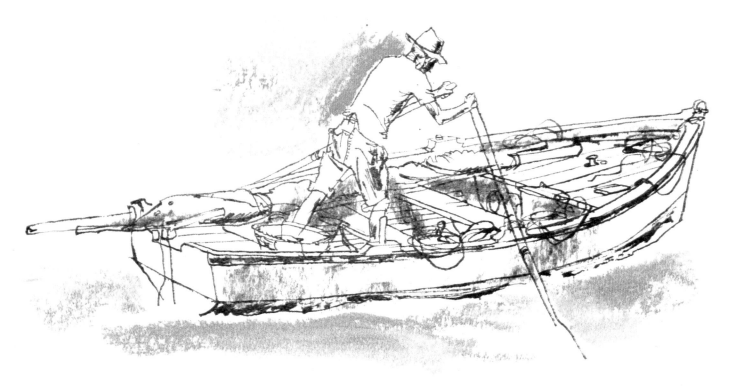

Hall of Fame 1983

FRANKLIN BOOTH (1874-1948)

Although the craft of wood engraving has now almost become extinct, it has had a venerable history going back to the origins of printing. At the time that Franklin Booth was a farm boy growing up in Indiana, the only illustrations he saw in books and magazines were still reproduced by that method of cutting away the wood block into finely spaced lines which would be inked and printed to simulate the tonal variations in the artist's original drawing or painting. Believing that the engraved lines were produced by pen and ink, he practiced endlessly to duplicate those delicate lines with a pen point, striving to become an artist himself. He also developed an unorthodox method of making detailed pencilling of only a small area and completing the rendering in pen and ink on a page otherwise containing only a generalized concept of the completed picture. As he later described his procedure, "My drawings are usually somewhat involved and a completed pencil drawing to begin with would become smudged in places in the process of inking other parts. I finish a section at a time and often this will appear in the midst of white paper with pencilled suggestions. This area also establishes values for the whole drawing. The starting point is usually a section showing the darkest darks, highest whites and greys . . ."*

The laboriously produced pictures look effortless; however, their skillfulness is entirely subordinated to the subject. It is in his picture concepts that Booth was unique. He was more concerned with ideas and ideals than in specifics. He took a long view that is an uplifting one, with a sensitive understanding and appreciation of nature as well as of man's architecture in his work. Much of his work was commissioned to illustrate poetry and editorials, but he also brought dignity and stature to a number of advertising clients.

His work shows us much about the man who lived by his classical beliefs in art as truth and beauty. As one of his students, I knew him to be guided by the same idealism in his personality. Never dogmatic, he was gentle in criticism, always encouraging and he taught most effectively by expecting much of us.

While our concepts of art and truth may have changed in these more pragmatic times, his kind of idealistic vision is still needed and can still inspire us as much as ever by its example.

Walt Reed

*Pen Technique by Franklin Booth, Frances Publishing Company, 1947.

Illustration: Franklin Booth
Courtesy Illustration House

Hamilton King Award

The Hamilton King Award is given each year for the finest illustration by a member of the Society of Illustrators. The 1983 award winner is Robert M. Cunningham.

1983 Hamilton King Award Jurors:

David Blossom
Paul Calle
Gerald McConnell
Wilson McLean
Charles Santore
Miriam Schottland
Daniel Schwartz
William Teason

Hamilton King Award Winners:

1965 Paul Calle
1966 Bernie Fuchs
1967 Mark English
1968 Robert Peak
1969 Alan Cober
1970 Ray Ameijide
1971 Miriam Schottland
1972 Charles Santore
1973 Dave Blossom
1974 Fred Otnes
1975 Carol Anthony
1976 Judith Jampel
1977 Leo & Diane Dillon
1978 Daniel Schwartz
1979 William Teason
1980 Wilson McLean
1981 Gerald McConnell
1982 Robert Heindel
1983 Robert Morris Cunningham

Hamilton King Award 1983

ROBERT MORRIS CUNNINGHAM
(b. 1924)
Interviewed by Art Weithas

Art Weithas: Congratulations on receiving the Hamilton King Award for 1983. It must be a nice feeling to receive a prestigious award like this, juried by your peers.

Bob Cunningham: Yes, it certainly is. I believe a compliment from your fellow artist is the best compliment you can get.

AW: For the record, can you provide some background material about yourself, i.e. where you were born, grew up, schools attended, avocations, etc., anything that might be of interest to a fellow artist or student.

BC: I was born in Herington, Kansas. At 12 moved to Kansas City, Kansas. Attended University of Kansas, Kansas City Art Institute and the Art Students League where I studied with Kuniyoshi, Corbino and Boss. My avocations are music, marine fish and photography.

AW: Your style of painting is so distinctive in its simplicity, can you give me some idea how you arrived at it?

BC: My style isn't something I decided to do. It just evolved. When I think about it, it probably was a personal revolt against a very literal background (drawing from plaster casts, etc.). Kuniyoshi once told me "You don't have to put a shadow in just because it's there". I did have to put it in. For years I had to put it in. Now I feel fairly free about manipulating the material. I spent many years reducing compositions of the masters to miniatures, simplifying them into small simple compositions.

AW: What artists had the greatest influence on your style?

BC: I had many favorite artists over the years. I don't believe I could name one that influenced me more than others.

AW: Your paintings always have a sun-drenched feeling of the outdoors about them . . . How did you arrive at this technique?

BC: By getting invited to a beautiful sun-drenched island.

AW: I understand that you spend a great deal of time in the Bahamas. Is it Eleuthra? Did the brilliant tropical colors and the clean open sky and water influence your color sense? You capture it so well in your paintings.

BC: Yes, it is Eleuthera at Governors Harbour and we go there everytime we are invited. The whole area is a visual feast.

AW: When Matisse and Dufy worked in the Mediterranean, their palettes suddenly exploded with color. Do you get the same reaction from painting in the Bahamas?

BC: All colors seem to be saturated and intense and it would be impossible not to be overwhelmed. It's the only place I've been where the colors match my emotions.

AW: How do you arrive at your color schemes?

BC: It's intuitive. No color is a color by itself. It is only in juxtaposition to another color that it assumes its hue. A picture is a continuing adjustment of one color to another.

AW: Do you use photographs as reference?

BC: Naturally. It is impossible to record a situation such as a race without recording it with a camera. I later rear-project and simplify the composition. I squint a lot.

AW: Is there any guidance or helpful suggestions that you would relay to students to help develop their own style of painting?

BC: I am not sure I'm the best person to give that advice. I seem to always do everything the hard way.

After the interview, we discussed painting and drawing in general and Bob produced a number of drawings that he had done of cadavers. They were large, done in charcoal pencil. They were exquisitely rendered with authority, discrimination and taste. I felt very privileged to see them. And we discussed the difference between drawing and painting. He feels that drawing can be compared to "A string quartet as opposed to the full orchestration of a painting". A delightful quote to end a very interesting interview.

Besides Robert Cunningham's Hamilton King Award in 1983, he has received gold medals from the Society of Illustrators in 1966, 67, 78, 80 and a silver medal award in 1983. Bob lives in Greenwich Village in New York City with his wife Jean, who is a fashion artist.

Illustration: Robert M. Cunningham for Boating Magazine

JURY

HARRY BENNETT, Chairman
Freelance illustrator. Romance paperback book covers. SI Annual
Exhibition award winner.

ROGER BLACK
Art director, The New York Times Magazine. Awards include Jerome
Snyder Memorial from SPD.

CHRIS HILL
Designer. Owner of Graphic Design for Marketing. Hill/A graphic
design group.

WENDELL MINOR
Freelance illustrator. Over 100 awards from organizations and
publications. Faculty member, SVA.

PAULA SCHER
Freelance art director. Awards from ADC, SI, AIGA, CA Magazine,
AD Magazine. 4 Grammy Award nominations for best album covers.

HODGES SOILEAU
Freelance illustrator.

EDWARD SOREL
Cartoonist and caricaturist. Winner of George Polk Award for satiric
drawing.

OTTO STORCH
Freelance designer/consultant art director. Over 500 awards. ADC Hall
of Fame.

ATTILA HEJJA
Freelance illustrator.

EDITORIAL

JURYING THE ANNUAL EXHIBITION: HOW IT WORKS

The most important function of the Annual Exhibition Past Chairmen's Committee is the selection of jurors which takes place approximately seven months prior to the actual jurying.

A large blackboard is set up with five vertical columns—four for the categories (Advertising, Editorial, Book & Institutional) and one in which to list diverse types of jurors. Every effort is made to create a good mix of illustrators and art directors with a wide range of tastes.

The first jurors selected are four Society of Illustrators members, each of whom acts as chairman of one of the categories. Eight additional jurors, including non-Society members, are then selected for each category. In order to avoid bias, jurors are placed in categories other than those from which their primary income is derived professionally. A period of three years must elapse before a juror may serve again. Jurors may not win awards in the category they are judging.

Jurying takes place during four evenings in October—one category a night. All published entries are set out in piles of black and white, 2-color, full color, and are also broken down according to size within that framework. After the jurors have completed viewing all the entries and have marked those which they feel qualify for the show, the staff sorts them into groups of "like" votes and those with the highest are brought back to be considered for awards.

During the initial voting, jurors are asked to vote silently, without discussion, but when the selection of awards gets underway, jurors are invited to express their views on why they think a certain piece merits an award.

The unpublished entries, submitted in slide form, are projected on a screen and voted on by means of a unique voting machine which enables each juror to cast his vote privately. Awards for unpublished pieces are selected the following week by the Balancing Jury.

The Balancing Jury is composed of the four Category Chairmen and two Past Chairmen. Since each artist accepted in the show is allowed no more than three pieces in a category and no more than five in the entire show (not counting award-winning pieces), it is the Balancing Jury's responsibility to whittle down those exceeding this number.

The Society of Illustrators takes great pride in the integrity with which this show has been run over the years and intends to maintain this high standard.

Arpi Ermoyan
EXECUTIVE DIRECTOR

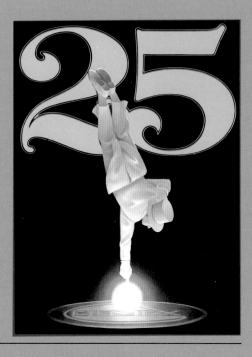

1

Artist: ROBERT GOLDSTROM
Art Director: Carveth Hilton Kramer
Magazine: Psychology Today

GOLD MEDAL

2

Artist: JOHN COLLIER
Art Director: Tina Adamek
Magazine: Postgraduate Medicine

SILVER MEDAL

3

Artist: BRAD HOLLAND
Art Director: Vincent Winter
Magazine: Inside Sports

SILVER MEDAL

4
Artist: STANISLAW ZAGORSKI
Art Director: Ken Smith
Client: Best of Business

5
Artist: THOMAS WOODRUFF
Art Director: Jaye Medalia
Magazine: Psychology Today

6

Artist: ROBERT GIUSTI   Art Director: Judy Garlan   Magazine: The Atlantic Monthly

7

Artist: ROBERT E. McGINNIS   Art Director: Lawrence A. Laukhuf   Magazine: Guideposts

8

Artist: JAMIE HOGAN
Art Director: Ronn Campisi
Magazine: Boston Globe

9
Artist: DANIEL MAFFIA
Art Director: Nancy Butkus
Magazine: California

Artist: CHRIS NOTARILE   Art Director: Rip Georges   Magazine: Playgirl

10

Artist: RICHARD ANDERSON
Art Director: Jerry Alten
Magazine: TV Guide

11

Artist: RICHARD HESS
Art Director: Jerry Alten
Magazine: TV Guide

Artist: ROGER HUYSSEN
Art Director: Richard Aloisio
Magazine: Inside Sports

14

Artist: BRAD HOLLAND   Art Director: Tom Staebler/Len Willis   Magazine: Playboy

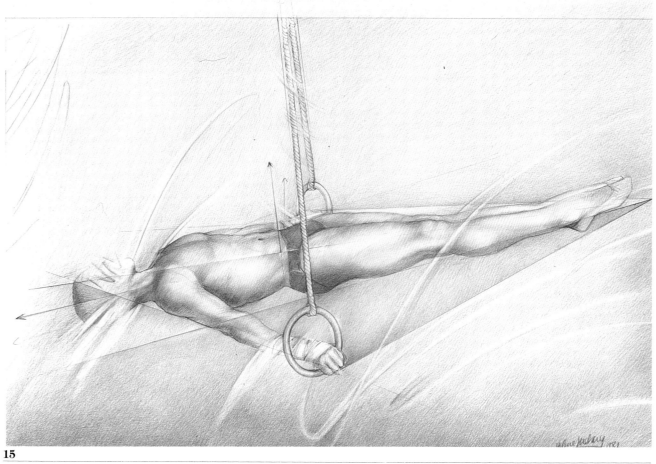

15

Artist: HELENE GUETARY   Art Director: Joe Brooks   Magazine: Penthouse

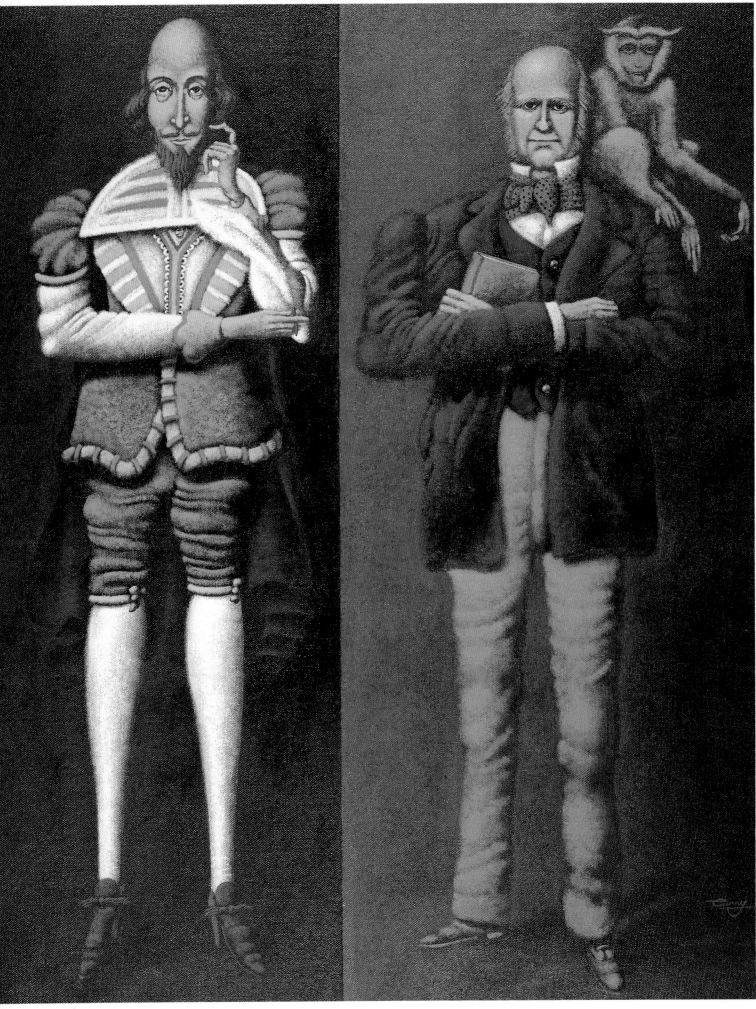

Artist: TOM CURRY   Art Director: Richard Payne   Magazine: Exxon USA

17
Artist: MARK ULRICH   Art Director: Mary Lynn Blasutta   Magazine: Ohio

18
Artist: GINI SHURTLEFF
Art Director: James Sarfati/Dale Moyer
Magazine: Scholastic Scope

19

Artist: HERB TAUSS   Art Director: Lawrence A. Laukhuf   Magazine: Guideposts

20

Artist: SKIP LIEPKE

21

Artist: DONALD STOLTENBERG   Art Director: Donald H. Duffy   Magazine: Reader's Digest

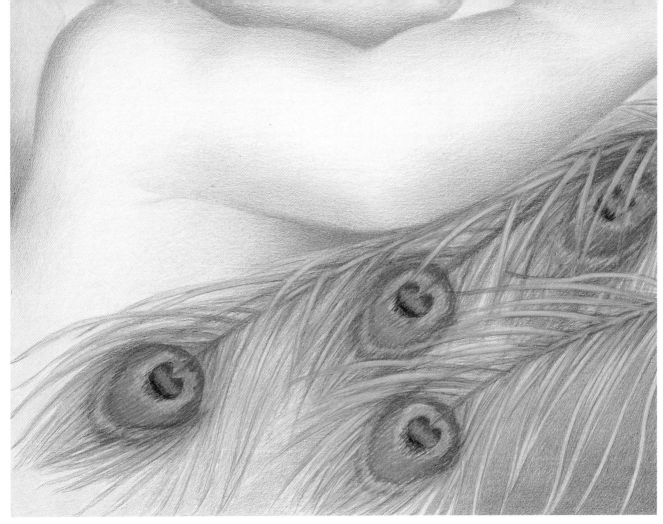

22

Artist: VICTORIA FAUST
Art Director: Judy Garlan
Magazine: The Atlantic Monthly

23

Artist: BARBARA NESSIM
Art Director: Diane Lamparon
Magazine: Ms.

Artist: JOHN BERKEY

Artist: JOHN BERKEY

26

Artist: RICHARD SCHLECHT   Art Director: Arnold C. Holeywell   Publisher: Time-Life Books

27

Artist: DANIEL SCHWARTZ   Art Director: Thomas R. Lunde   Magazine: Newsweek

28

Artist: JOHN CRAIG
Art Director: Theo Kouvatsos
Magazine: Playboy

29

Artist: ROBERT M. CUNNINGHAM   Art Director: Brian Canniff   Magazine: Boating   HAMILTON KING AWARD

30

Artist: MICHAEL DUDASH   Art Director: Gary Gretter   Magazine: Sports Afield

31

Artist: DAVID LEVINE   Art Director: Judy Garlan   Magazine: The Atlantic Monthly

32

Artist: ARTHUR SHILSTONE
Art Director: Larry Taylor
Magazine: Gray's Sporting Journal

33
Artist: RICHARD HESS
Art Director: Jerry Alten
Magazine: TV Guide

34
Artist: GARY KELLEY
Art Director: Gary Bernloehr
Magazine: Florida Trend

35

Artist: RONALD SHERR   Art Director: Rudolph Hoglund   Magazine: Time

36

Artist: SCOTT NEARY
Art Director: Janet Perr
Magazine: Rolling Stone

37

Artist: FRANK MORRIS
Art Director: Margaret Joskow
Magazine: Newsweek

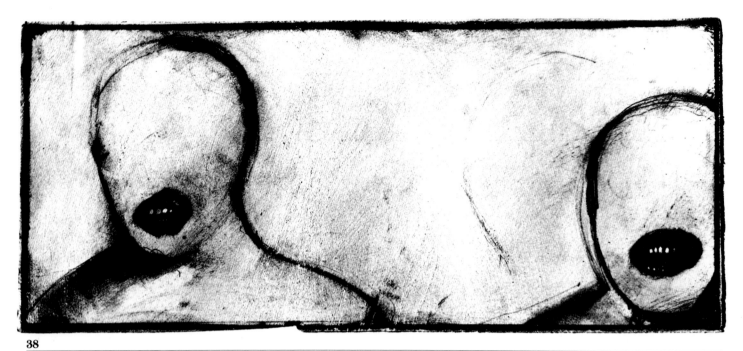

38

Artist: MATT MAHURIN   Art Director: Tim Rutten   Client: Los Angeles Times

39

Artist: CATHIE BLECK   Art Director: James Noel Smith   Client: Dallas Times Herald

40

Artist: BOBBI TULL
Art Director: Ed Schneider
Magazine: Washington Post

Artist: SCOTT REYNOLDS
Art Director: Fred Woodward
Magazine: Westward

43
Artist: GUY BILLOUT
Art Director: Judy Garlan
Magazine: The Atlantic Monthly

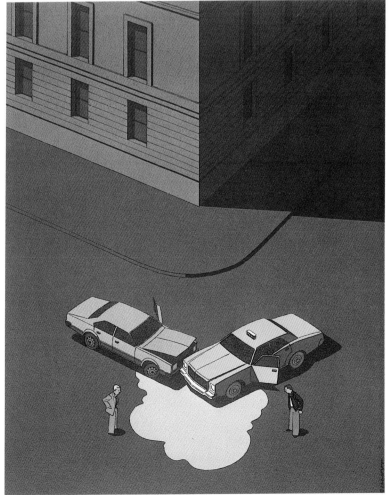

41
Artist: DENNIS ZIEMIENSKI
Art Director: Gary Bernloehr
Magazine: Florida Trend

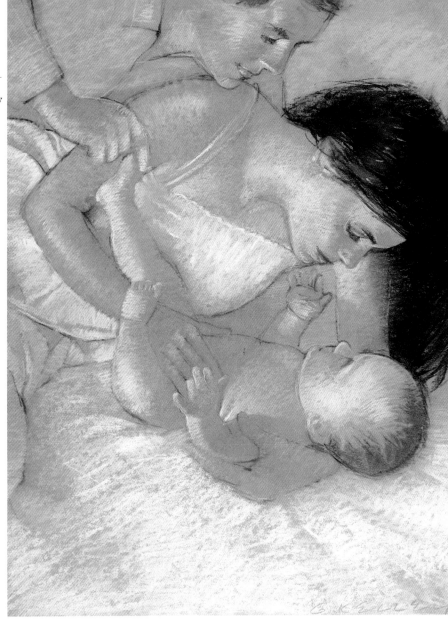

44
Artist: GARY KELLEY
Art Director: Ken Smith/Susan Lyday
Client: Pre-Parent Adviser

45
Artist: JACK ENDEWELT
Art Director: Murray J. Miller
Magazine: Reader's Digest

Artist: WENDELL MINOR   Art Director: Modesto Torre   Magazine: McCall's

47

Artist: BILL DULA
Art Director: Sheldon Hofmann
Client: "Today" Show

48

Artist: JOHN CRAIG   Art Director: Barbara Koster   Magazine: Passages

Artist: ALAN E. COBER   Art Director: Don Owens   Magazine: Westward

Artist: TOM CURRY
Art Director: Greg Paul/Tom Curry
Magazine: Cleveland Plain Dealer

51

Artist: LEE A. BOYNTON   Art Director: Ed Schneider   Magazine: The Washington Post

52

Artist: BURT SILVERMAN   Art Director: Murray Belsky   Magazine: American Heritage

53

Artist: ROBERT GIUSTI
Art Director: Judy Garlan
Magazine: The Atlantic Monthly

54

Artist: JERRY TIRITILLI
Art Director: Jeffrey Hapner
Magazine: Joystik

55

Artist: MICHAEL WHELAN
Art Director: Don Myrus
Magazine: Omni

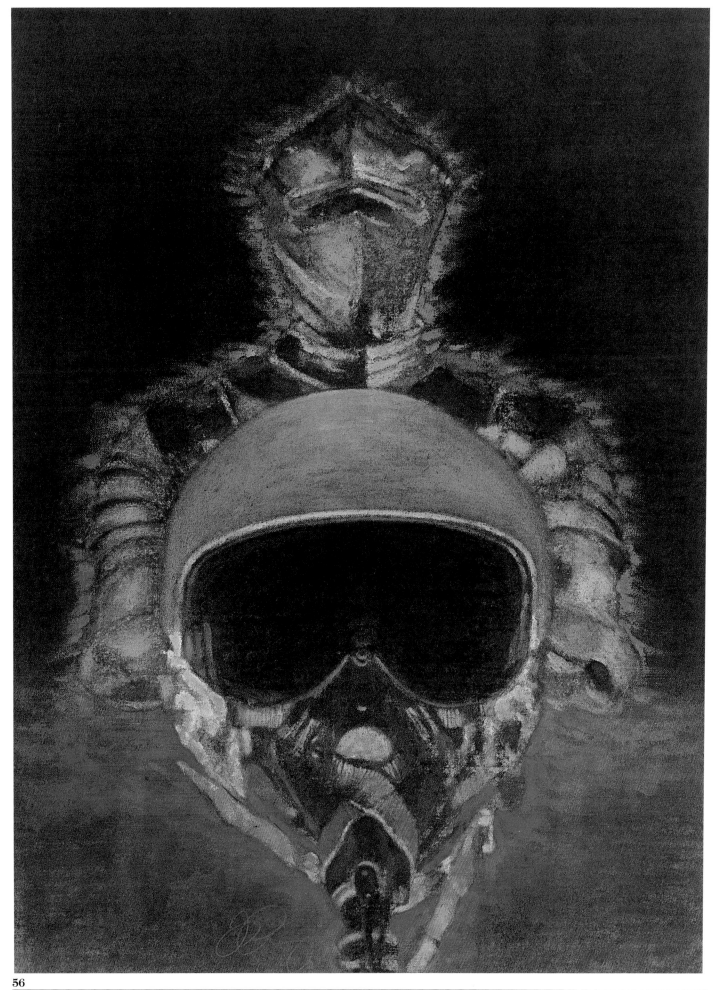

Artist: JACK PARDUE   Art Director: Bill Ford   Magazine: Air Force

Artist: GUY BILLOUT   Art Director: Judy Garlan   Magazine: The Atlantic Monthly

58
Artist: JAMES McMULLAN
Art Director: Robert Best
Magazine: New York

59
Artist: BERNIE FUCHS
Art Director: Harvey Grut
Magazine: Sports Illustrated

60

Artist: DAVID LESH
Art Director: Eileen Divine/Sherry Brooks
Client: International Computer Programs

61

Artist: MARSHALL ARISMAN
Art Director: Louise Kollenbaum
Magazine: Mother Jones

62

Artist: JOHN VARGO
Art Director: Donald H. Duffy
Magazine: Reader's Digest

Artist: GARY RUDDELL   Art Director: Skip Williamson   Magazine: Playboy

64
Artist: FRED OTNES
Art Director: Joe Brooks
Magazine: Penthouse

65
Artist: EUGENE MIHAESCO
Art Director: Rudolph Hoglund
Magazine: Time

2:05 and holding - with a 1 hour delay - 5:40 AM - waiting for the suit up - astronauts now up 10 mins at 6:20 AM Cape Canaveral Kennedy Space Center 22 Mar
Alan E. Cober

66

Artist: ALAN E. COBER
Art Director: Bruce Sanders/Robert Schulman
Client: Technology Illustrated/NASA

67

Artist: DAVID LEVINE
Art Director: Judy Garlan
Magazine: The Atlantic Monthly

68

Artist: EUGENE MIHAESCO
Art Director: Arturo Cazeneuve
Magazine: Time

69

Artist: WALT SPITZMILLER   Art Director: Harvey Grut   Magazine: Sports Illustrated

70

Artist: WALT SPITZMILLER   Art Director: Harvey Grut   Magazine: Sports Illustrated

71

Artist: ELWOOD SMITH
Art Director: Fred Woodward
Client: Dallas Times Herald

73

Artist: FRANCES JETTER
Art Director: Patrick Flynn
Magazine: The Progressive

74

Artist: R.J. SHAY
Art Director: R.J. Shay
Client: St. Louis Post Dispatch

72

Artist: EDWARD SOREL
Art Director: Rudy Hoglund
Magazine: Time

75
Artist: BRALDT BRALDS
Art Director: Rudy Hoglund
Magazine: Time International

76
Artist: JOHN A. GURCHE
Art Director: John A. Gurche
Client: Smithsonian

Detail

77

Artist: STEVEN GUARNACCIA
Art Director: Michael Grossman
Magazine: National Lampoon

79

Artist: ROBERT E. McGINNIS   Art Director: Bruce Danbrot   Magazine: Good Housekeeping

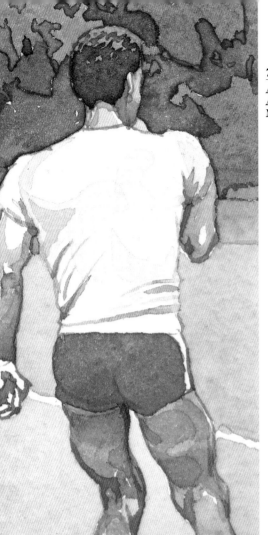

78
Artist: JAMES McMULLAN
Art Director: Robert Best
Magazine: New York

80
Artist: WILLIAM TEASON

81

Artist: DANIEL SCHWARTZ
Art Director: Rudolph Hoglund
Magazine: Time

82

Artist: RICHARD AMSEL
Art Director: Jerry Alten
Magazine: TV Guide

Artist: EDWARD SOREL
Art Director: Christian von Rosenvinge
Magazine: Columbia Journalism Review

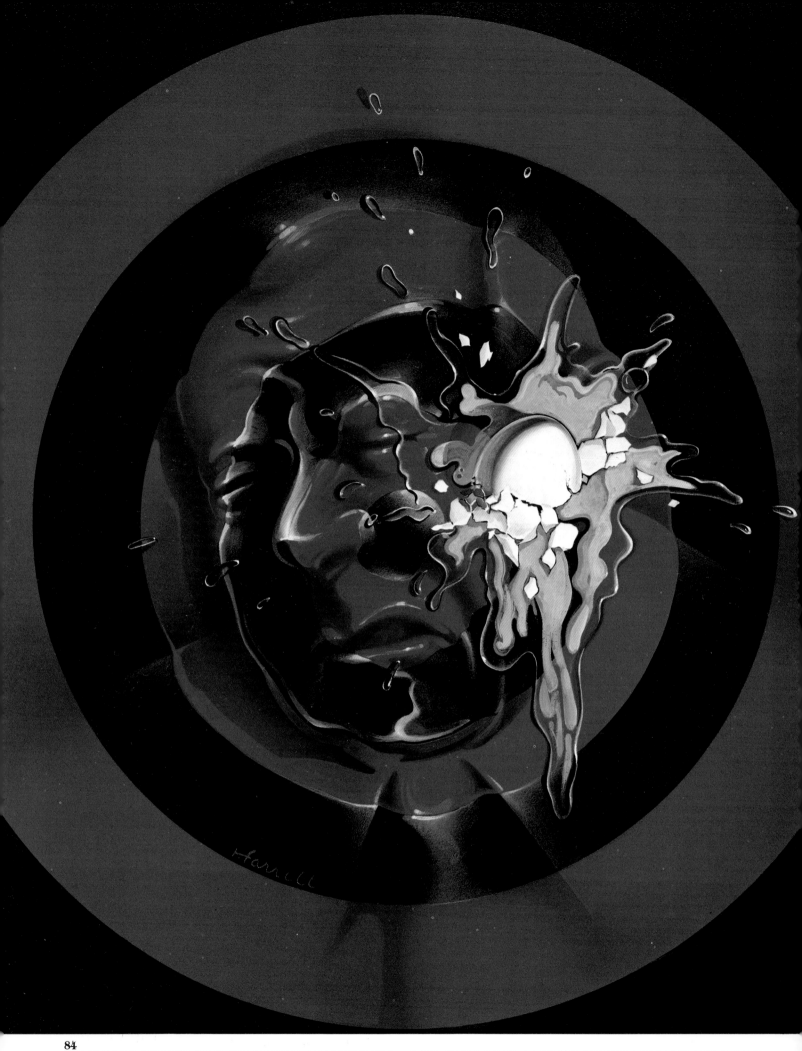

Artist: RICHARD B. FARRELL   Art Director: Wayne Burkhart   Magazine: John Deere Journal

85

Artist: KATHY JEFFERS
Art Director: Andrew Steigmeier
Magazine: Mechanix Illustrated

86

Artist: BOB SELBY
Art Director: Raymond Lomax
Magazine: Providence Journal

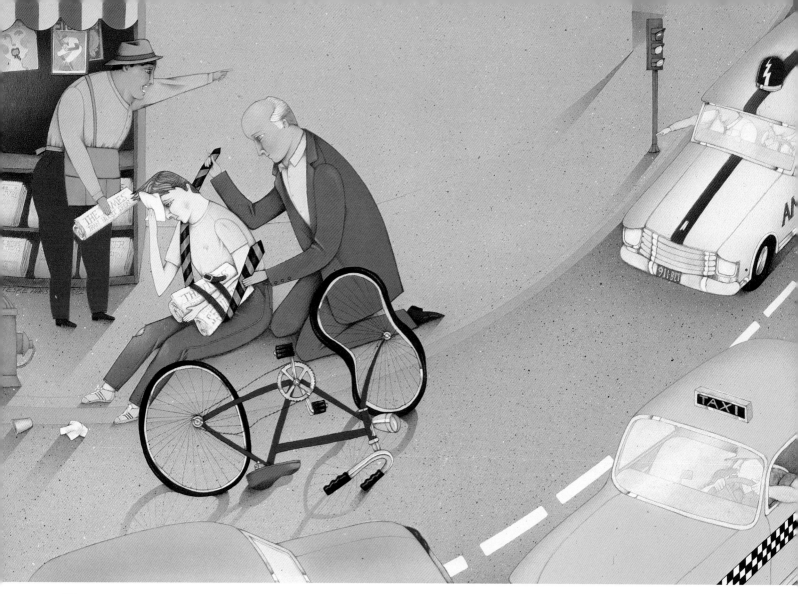

87
Artist: DIANE TESKE HARRIS
Art Director: Jim Walsh
Magazine: Emergency Medicine

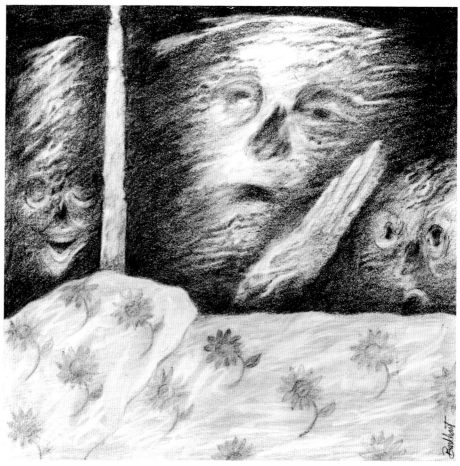

88
Artist: ROGER BURKHART
Art Director: James Noel Smith
Client: Dallas Times Herald

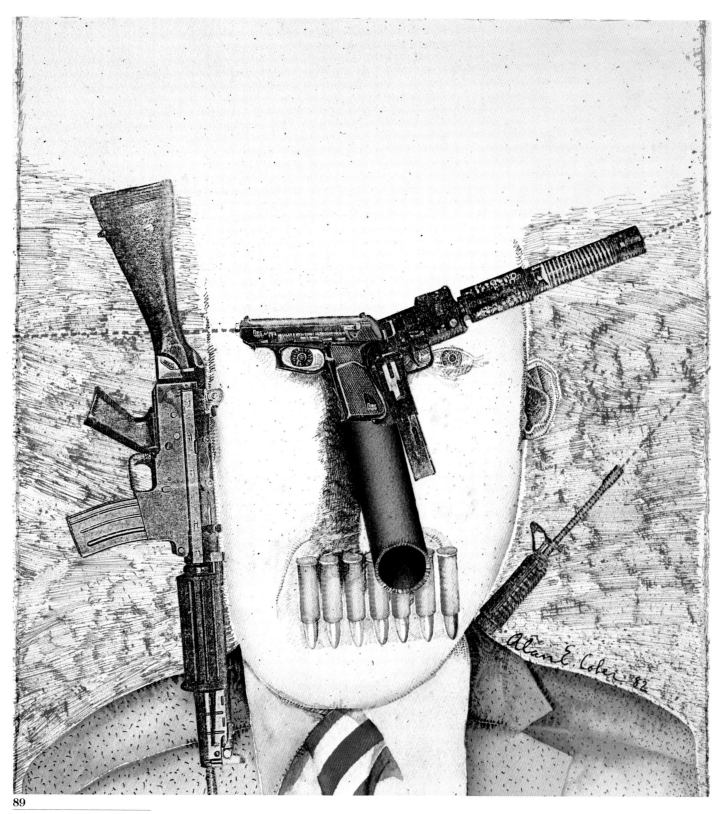

89

Artist: ALAN E. COBER
Art Director: Don Owens
Client: Dallas Times Herald

90

Artist: STANLEY MELTZOFF
Art Director: Howard E. Paine
Magazine: National Geographic

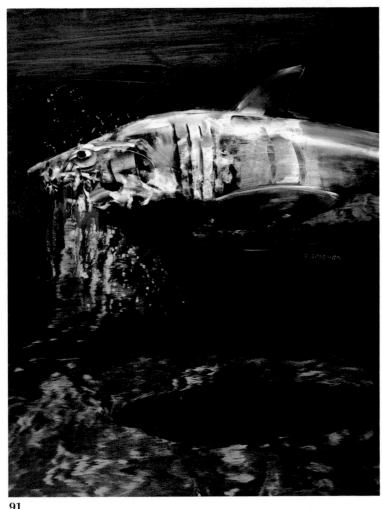

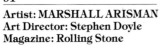

91

Artist: MARSHALL ARISMAN
Art Director: Stephen Doyle
Magazine: Rolling Stone

92

Artist: STANLEY MELTZOFF
Art Director: Howard E. Paine
Magazine: National Geographic

93

Artist: STANLEY MELTZOFF
Art Director: Howard E. Paine
Magazine: National Geographic

94

Artist: FRANCES JETTER
Art Director: Ronn Campisi
Magazine: The Boston Globe

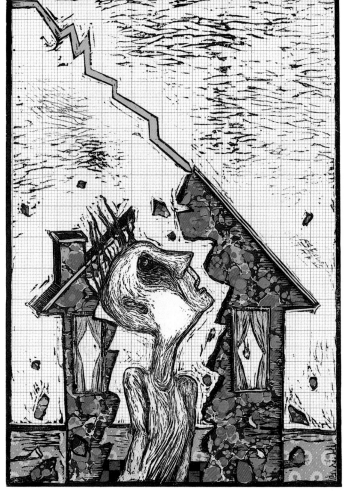

95
Artist: FRANCES JETTER
Art Director: Kati Korpijaako
Magazine: New Jersey Monthly

Artist: BRAD HOLLAND   Art Director: Paul Hardy/Miles Abernathy   Magazine: Attenzione

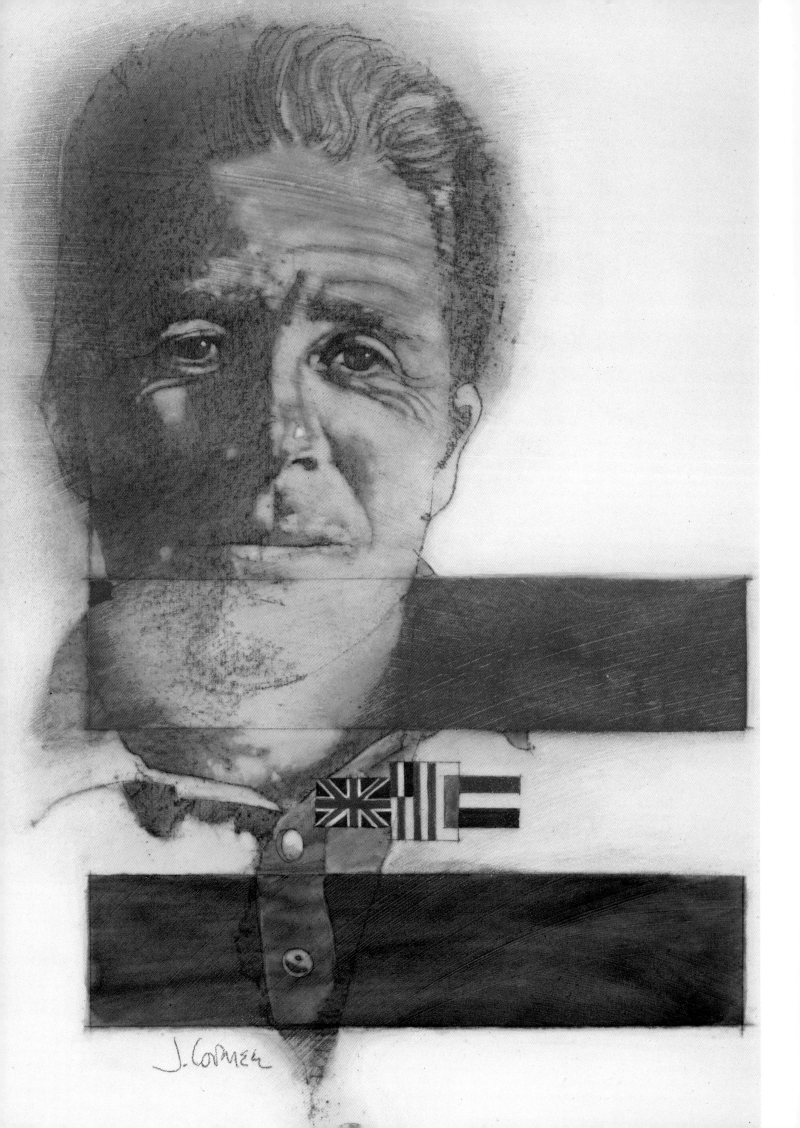

J. Cormier

The West Side's Hottest Spot, by Jennifer Allen

Reaganomics After Stockman, by Michael Kramer

NEW YORK.

Living on the Edge

Denise Cohen's Fatal Courtship With Danger

By Rinker Buck

98

Artist: BURT SILVERMAN
Art Director: Robert Best
Magazine: New York

99

Artist: BURT SILVERMAN
Art Director: Leonard Wolfe
Magazine: Discover

97

Artist: JEFF CORNELL   Art Director: Daryl F. Herrmann   Magazine: Golf

·CHICKINOCEROS·

100
Artist: WENDELL MINOR
Art Director: Alice Degenhardt
Magazine: Creative Living

101
Artist: SEYMOUR CHWAST
Art Director: Ronn Campisi
Magazine: The Boston Globe

102
Artist: TOM CURRY
Art Director: Fred Woodward
Magazine: "D"

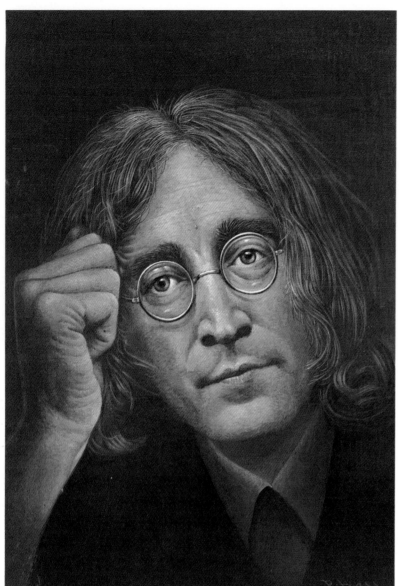

103
Artist: RICHARD HESS
Art Director: Jerry Alten
Magazine: TV Guide

104
Artist: STEVE MENDELSON
Art Director: Robert Barkin
Magazine: The Washington Post

105

Artist: JOHN A. WILSON   Art Director: John A. Wilson/Dick Reeves

106

Artist: CHUCK SLACK   Art Director: Skip Williamson   Magazine: Playboy

107
Artist: STAN HUNTER
Art Director: Ed Werth
Client: Doubleday

108
Artist: CAT BENNETT
Art Director: Valerie Bessette
Magazine: Boston

109

Artist: TOM INGHAM
Art Director: Tom Staebler/Bob Post
Magazine: Playboy

110

Artist: **MARK MAREK**
Art Director: Michael Grossman
Magazine: National Lampoon

111

Artist: **MARK MAREK**
Art Director: Michael Grossman
Magazine: National Lampoon

Artist: LOU BROOKS
Art Director: Steve Duckett
Magazine: Florida Trend

Boa Constrictor

Artist: DUGALD STERMER
Art Director: Nancy Butkus
Magazine: New West

Artist: DUGALD STERMER
Art Director: Nancy Butkus
Magazine: New West

113

Artist: JACK UNRUH
Art Director: Joe Connolly
Magazine: Boy's Life

116

Artist: EUGENE MIHAESCO   Art Director: Irene Ramp   Magazine: Time

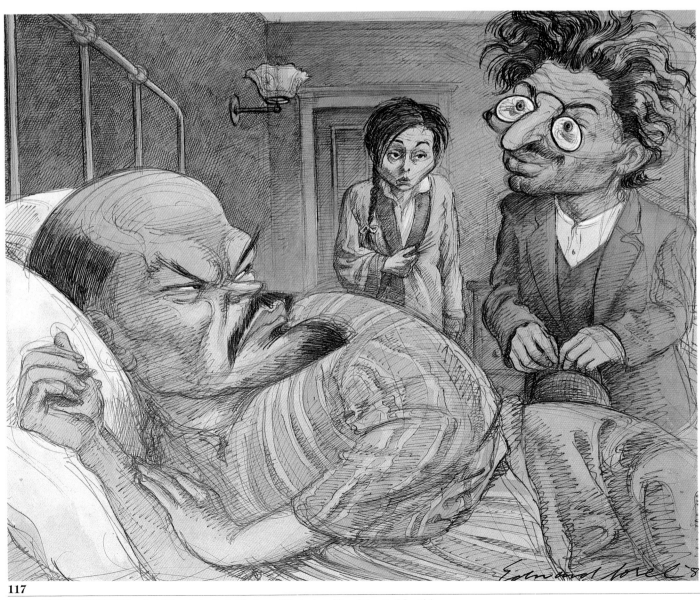

117

Artist: EDWARD SOREL   Art Director: Judy Garlan   Magazine: The Atlantic Monthly

118

Artist: BILL VUKSANOVICH

119

Artist: ROBERT M. CUNNINGHAM
Art Director: Harvey Grut
Magazine: Sports Illustrated

120

Artist: DOUGLAS SMITH
Art Director: Ronn Campisi
Magazine: The Boston Globe

121

Artist: ELWOOD SMITH
Art Director: Michael Grossman
Magazine: National Lampoon

125

Artist: DANIEL MAFFIA
Art Director: Judy Garlan
Magazine: The Atlantic Monthly

126

Artist: ROBERT HUNT
Art Director: Howard Shintaku
Client: California Today

Artist: **MARSHALL ARISMAN**
Art Director: Greg Paul
Magazine: Cleveland Plain Dealer

128

Artist: ED VEBELL
Art Director: Donald H. Duffy
Magazine: Reader's Digest

129
Artist: CARLOS LLERENA AGUIRRE
Art Director: Janet Froelich
Client: Daily News

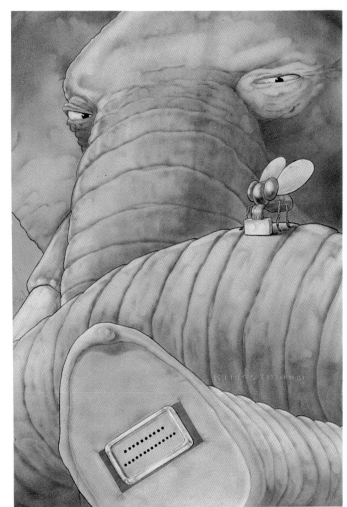

130
Artist: JIM KINGSTON
Art Director: Nick Dankowitch
Magazine: Industry Week

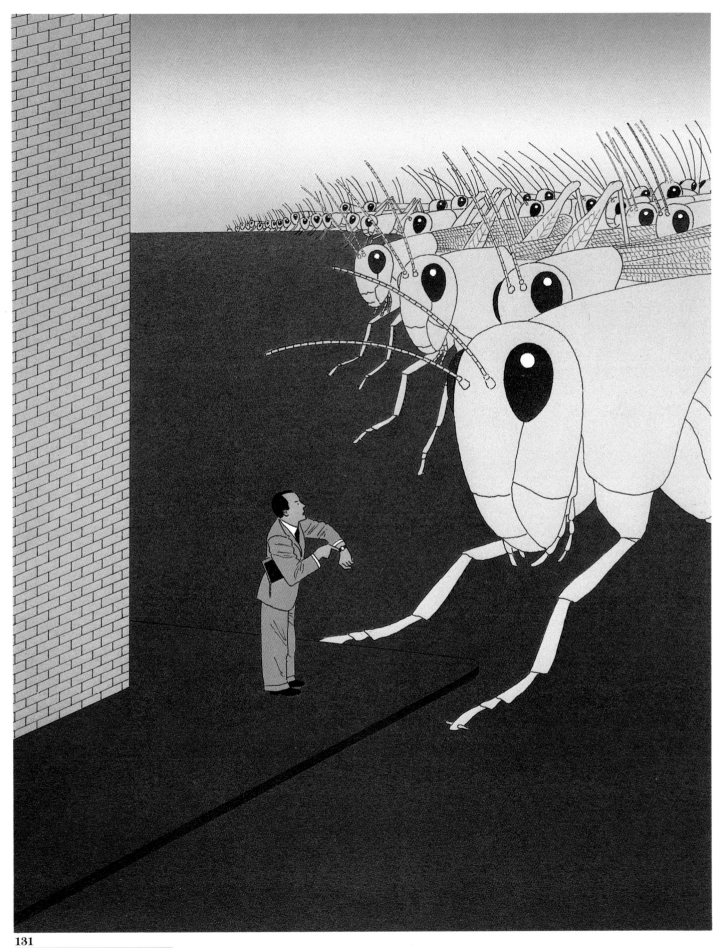

Artist: GUY BILLOUT
Art Director: Judy Garlan
Magazine: The Atlantic Monthly

Artist: MEL ODOM
Art Director: Tom Staebler/Kerig Pope
Magazine: Playboy

Artist: BARBARA NESSIM   Art Director: Daniel Grant/Elliot Barowitz   Magazine: Art Workers News

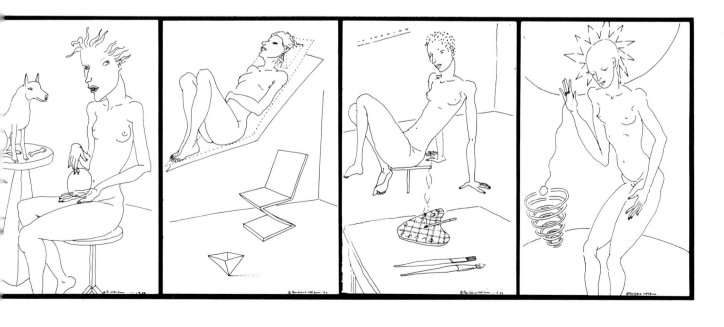

Artist: DOUGLAS SMITH
Art Director: Valerie Bessette
Magazine: Boston

137
Artist: GARY PANTER
Art Director: Alfred Zelcer
Magazine: Philadelphia

135

Artist: MEL FURUKAWA
Art Director: Brad Pallas
Client: Channels of Communication

138
Artist: MARVIN MATTELSON
Art Director: Joe Brooks
Magazine: Penthouse

139
Artist: DAVID LEVINE
Art Director: Judy Garlan
Magazine: The Atlantic Monthly

Artist: BRAD HOLLAND
Art Director: Peter Hudson
Magazine: Technology Illustrated

141

Artist: TOM EVANS
Art Director: Stan McCray
Magazine: Houston City

Artist: BRALDT BRALDS   Art Director: Walter Herdeg   Magazine: Graphis

143
Artist: CHARLES REID
Art Director: Gary Gretter
Magazine: Sports Afield

Artist: SHANNON STIRNWEIS   Art Director: Victor J. Closi   Magazine: Field and Stream

Artist: WALT SPITZMILLER   Art Director: Harvey Grut   Magazine: Sports Illustrated

146

Artist: SCOTT REYNOLDS
Art Director: Fred Woodward
Magazine: Westward

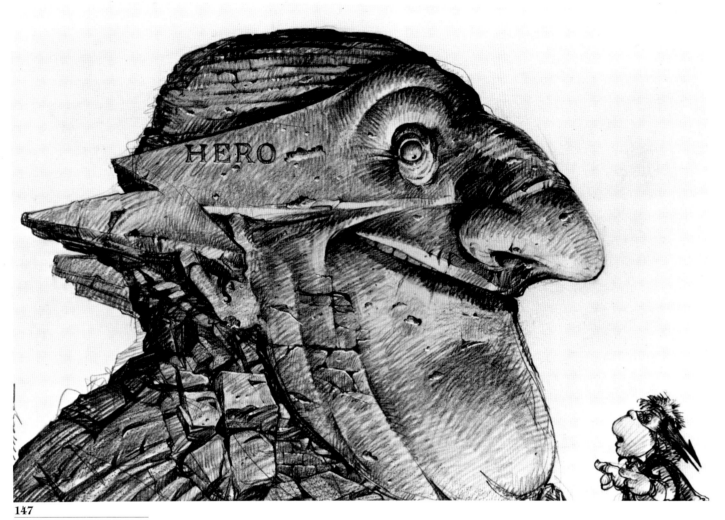

147

Artist: BILL MAYER
Art Director: Peter Hudson
Magazine: Atlanta

148
Artist: RICHARD SPARKS
Art Director: Richard Aloisio
Magazine: Inside Sports

149
Artist: MICHAEL DUDASH
Art Director: Jerry Alten
Magazine: TV Guide

150
Artist: BERNIE FUCHS
Art Director: Harvey Grut
Magazine: Sports Illustrated

151
Artist: MICHAEL DUDASH
Art Director: Jerry Alten
Magazine: TV Guide

Artist: HOVIK DILAKIAN   Art Director: Dale Moyer/Joe Borzetta   Magazine: Electronic Learning

153
Artist: MARK ULRICH
Art Director: Mary Lynn Blasutta
Magazine: Ohio

154

Artist: LONNI SUE JOHNSON   Art Director: Tom Lennon   Magazine: Emergency Medicine

155

Artist: ROBERT M. CUNNINGHAM
Art Director: Harvey Grut
Magazine: Sports Illustrated

156

Artist: RAUL DEL RIO
Art Director: Hal Silverman
Magazine: California Living

JURY

KO NODA, Chairman
Graphic designer. President, Ko Noda & Associates.

PAUL BACON
Designer/illustrator. Paul Bacon Studios, Inc.

SEYMOUR CHWAST
Graphic designer/illustrator. Director of Pushpin, Lubalin, Peckolick.
ADC Hall of Fame. St. Gauden's Medal from Cooper Union.

ROBERT T. HANDVILLE
Freelance illustrator. Awards from American Watercolor Society,
National Academy. Faculty member, FIT.

H. TOM HALL
Freelance illustrator.

JACQUI MORGAN
Freelance illustrator/painter. Exhibited in U.S. and Europe.

GEORGE TSCHERNY
Graphic Designer. George Tscherny, Inc. Permanent Collection,
Museum of Modern Art.

JACK UNRUH
Freelance illustrator.

DON WELLER
Freelance illustrator/designer. Awards for illustration, graphic design
and art direction.

BOOK

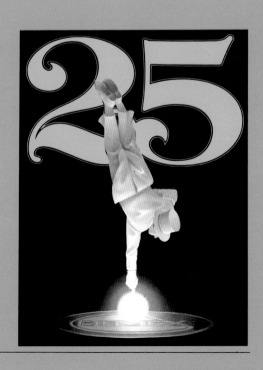

Artist: RICH McCOLLUM   Art Director: William Gregory   Publisher: Reader's Digest   SILVER MEDAL

Artist: **JOHN COLLIER**   Art Director: Alex Jay   Publisher: **Byron Preiss Visual Publications, Inc.**   **SILVER MEDAL**

159

Artist: BRALDT BRALDS
Art Director: Lidia Ferrara
Publisher: Alfred A. Knopf, Inc.

SILVER MEDAL

160

Artist: ALAN MAGEE
Art Director: Milton Charles
Publisher: Pocket Books

161

Artist: HERB TAUSS
Art Director: Michael Mendelsohn
Publisher: The Franklin Library

162

Artist: AMY HILL
Art Director: Louise Fili
Publisher: Pantheon Books

163

Artist: MICHAEL DAVID BROWN
Art Director: Bob Scales
Client: Outlook Review

164

Artist: MICHAEL DAVID BROWN
Art Director: Bob Scales
Client: Outlook Review

165

Artist: MICHAEL DAVID BROWN
Art Director: Bob Scales
Client: Outlook Review

166
Artist: JOSEPH A. SMITH
Art Director: Patrick Cunningham
Publisher: Harry N. Abrams, Inc.

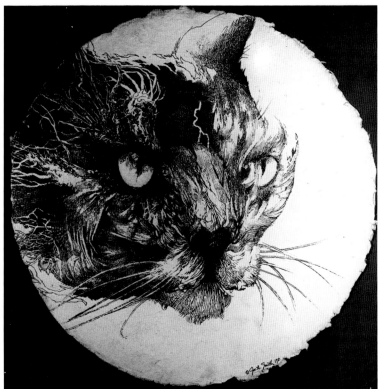

167
Artist: ROBERT GOLDSTROM
Art Director: Lynn Hollyn
Publisher: Workman

168

Artist: KATHLYN TENGA

169
Artist: STEVE KARCHIN
Art Director: Don Munson
Publisher: Ballantine/Del Rey

170
Artist: JIM SPANFELLER
Art Director: Michael Mendelsohn
Publisher: The Franklin Library

Artist: BASCOVE
Art Director: Dick Adleson
Publisher: Viking Penguin, Inc.

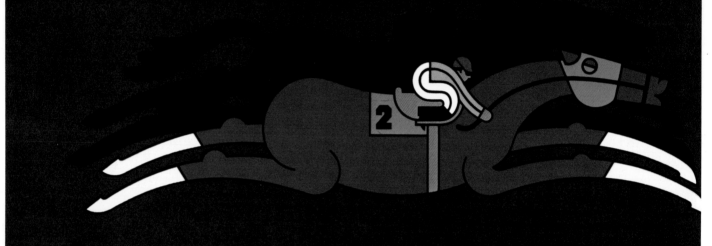

TWICE SHY

DICK FRANCIS

DICK FRANCIS

TWICE SHY

PUTNAM

Artist: BRIAN BOYD
Art Director: Brian Boyd
Publisher: G.P. Putnam & Sons

173
Artist: BRALDT BRALDS
Art Director: Lidia Ferrara
Publisher: Alfred A. Knopf, Inc.

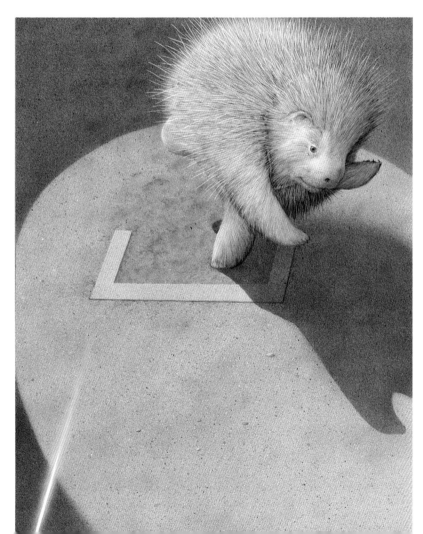

174
Artist: ERICK INGRAHAM
Art Director: Cynthia Basil
Publisher: Morrow Junior Books

175

Artist: JOHN MARTINEZ
Art Director: Louise Fili
Publisher: Pantheon Books

176
Artist: LONNI SUE JOHNSON
Art Director: Louis Fili
Publisher: Pantheon Books

177
Artist: RITA GRASSO
Art Director: William Luckey/Joy Chu
Publisher: David R. Godine

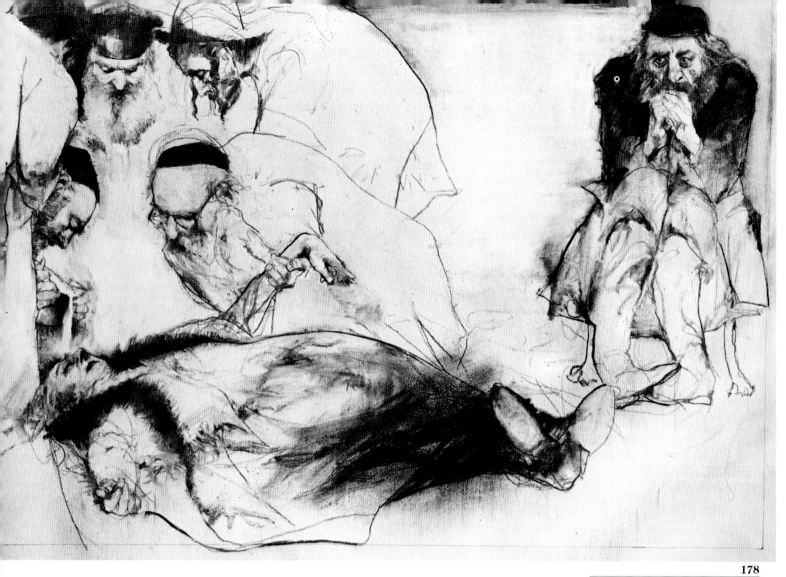

178
Artist: HERB TAUSS
Art Director: Michael Mendelsohn
Publisher: The Franklin Library

179
Artist: JOHN RUSH
Art Director: Don Munson
Publisher: Ballantine Books

180

Artist: BARRON STOREY
Art Director: Milton Charles
Publisher: Pocket Books

181

Artist: JIM MAZZOTTA
Art Director: Jim Mazzotta
Publisher: Soggy Cracker Press

182

Artist: PETER McCAFFREY

183

Artist: MURRAY TINKELMAN
Art Director: Art Weithas
Client: Society of Illustrators

184

Artist: ROBERT HEINDEL
Art Director: Soren Noring
Publisher: Reader's Digest

185
Artist: KAREN FARYNIAK

186
Artist: ROBERT HEINDEL
Art Director: Soren Noring
Publisher: Reader's Digest

187

Artist: JILL BAUMAN

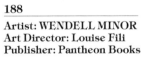

188

Artist: WENDELL MINOR
Art Director: Louise Fili
Publisher: Pantheon Books

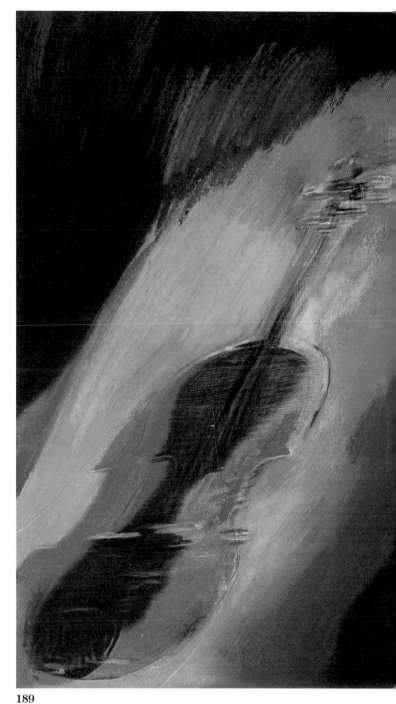

189

Artist: JANE STERRETT
Art Director: Kiffi Diamond
Client: G. Schirmer

193
Artist: ROBERT RODRIGUEZ
Art Director: Craig Butler
Client: L.A. Workbook

194
Artist: CHARLES MIKOLAYCAK
Art Director: Barbara G. Hennessy
Publisher: Viking Penguin, Inc.

195
Artist: CAROL WALD
Art Director: Jack Tauss/Joanne Giaquinto
Publisher: The Franklin Library

196

Artist: MARIA HORVATH   Art Director: Alan Benjamin   Publisher: MacMillan

197

Artist: KINUKO CRAFT   Art Director: Gene Mydlowski   Publisher: Berkley Books

198
Artist: LESLIE ROBIN   Art Director: Jim Plumeri   Publisher: New American Library

199
Artist: **RICHARD HARVEY**   Art Director: William Gregory   Publisher: Reader's Digest

200
Artist: BASCOVE
Art Director: Judith Loeser
Publisher: Random House

201
Artist: CHRISTOPHER BLOSSOM
Art Director: Len Leone
Publisher: Bantam Books

202
Artist: ROBERT E. McGINNIS
Art Director: Jim Plumeri
Publisher: New American Library

203
Artist: BOB LAPSLEY
Art Director: Jim Plumeri
Publisher: New American Library

204
Artist: SKIP LIEPKE
Art Director: Michael Mendelsohn
Publisher: The Franklin Library

205

Artist: HIRAM RICHARDSON
Art Director: Jerry Pfeifer
Publisher: Popular Library, Fawcett Books

206
Artist: JAVIER ROMERO

207
Artist: JOHN JUDE PALENCAR
Art Director: Byron Preiss/John Jude Palencar
Publisher: Bantam Books

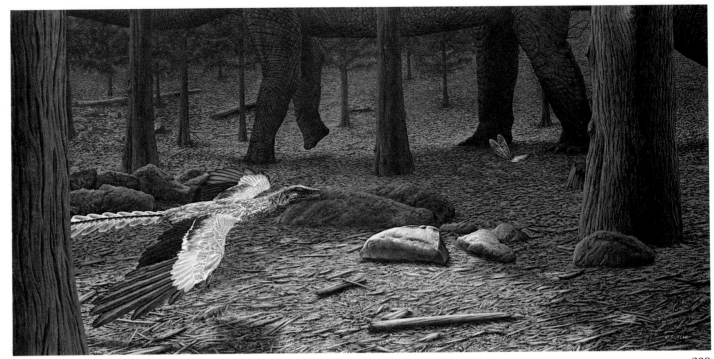

208

Artist: JOHN A. GURCHE
Art Director: Lynn Komai
Publisher: Smithsonian Books

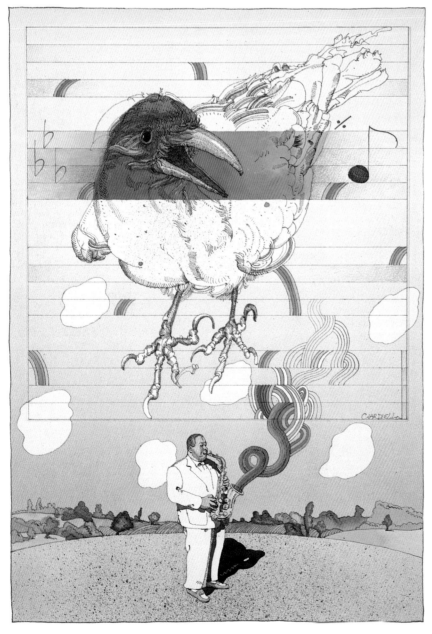

209

Artist: JOE CIARDIELLO

Artist: JON GOODELL
Art Director: Tom von Der Linn
Publisher: Reader's Digest

211

Artist: JAMES McMULLAN
Art Director: Nancy Etheredge
Publisher: E.P. Dutton

Artist: ROBERT HEINDEL   Art Director: Soren Noring   Publisher: Reader's Digest

213

Artist: DON BRAUTIGAM
Art Director: Jim Plumeri
Publisher: New American Library

214
Artist: LEO and DIANE DILLON
Art Director: Don Munson/Alex Jay
Publisher: Byron Preiss Visual Publications, Inc.

215
Artist: KINUKO CRAFT
Art Director: Barbara Bertoli
Publisher: Avon Books

Artist: HERB TAUSS   Art Director: Marion Davis   Publisher: Reader's Digest

Artist: SUSAN STILLMAN   Art Director: Nancy Etheredge   Publisher: E.P. Dutton

Artist: DAVID FRAMPTON
Art Director: Martha Lehtola Swanson
Publisher: Apple-Wood Books

Artist: MARC BROWN   Art Director: Atha Tehon   Publisher: Dial Books for Young Readers

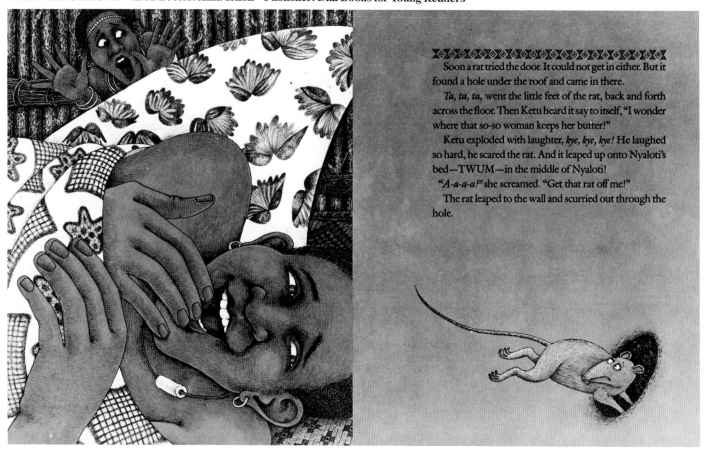

Soon a rat tried the door. It could not get in either. But it found a hole under the roof and came in there.

Ta, ta, ta, went the little feet of the rat, back and forth across the floor. Then Ketu heard it say to itself, "I wonder where that so-so woman keeps her butter!"

Ketu exploded with laughter, *kye, kye, kye!* He laughed so hard, he scared the rat. And it leaped up onto Nyaloti's bed—TWUM—in the middle of Nyaloti!

"*A-a-a-a!*" she screamed. "Get that rat off me!"

The rat leaped to the wall and scurried out through the hole.

Artist: WENDELL MINOR   Art Director: Frank Metz   Publisher: Summit Books

221

Artist: JOHN ALCORN
Art Director: Lidia Ferrara
Publisher: Alfred A. Knopf, Inc.

222

Artist: GLENN HARRINGTON
Art Director: Matt Tepper
Publisher: Avon Books

223
Artist: DAVID MONTIEL
Art Director: Judith Loeser
Publisher: Vintage Books

224
Artist: KAZUHIKO SANO
Art Director: Jerry Pfeifer
Client: CBS Publications

225
Artist: IZUMI INOUE
Art Director: Bob Feldgus
Publisher: Scholastic, Inc.

226
Artist: CARTER JONES

Sometimes at night I find
myself grasping to feel

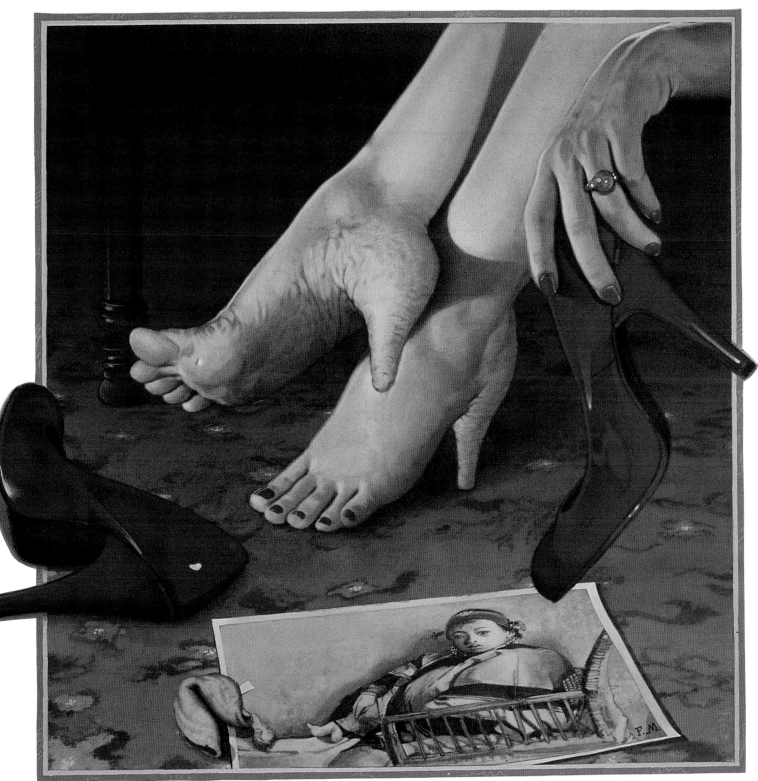

227

Artist: FRANK MORRIS
Art Director: Frank Metz
Publisher: Simon & Schuster

228

Artist: PETER COX
Art Director: Don Munson
Publisher: Ballantine/Del Ray

229

Artist: LEO and DIANE DILLON
Art Director: Len Leone
Publisher: Bantam Books

230

Artist: FREDERICKA RIBES
Art Director: Milton Charles
Publisher: Pocket Books

231

Artist: FREDERICKA RIBES
Art Director: Milton Charles
Publisher: Pocket Books

232
Artist: BOB ZIERING
Art Director: Char Lappan
Publisher: Little Brown & Co.

Bad Dogs
John S.P. Walker

233
Artist: JOHN S.P. WALKER
Art Director: Betty Anderson
Publisher: Alfred A. Knopf, Inc.

Artist: JOHN M. THOMPSON **Art Director: Len Leone** **Publisher: Bantam Books**

235
Artist: WENDELL MINOR
Art Director: Lidia Ferrara
Publisher: Alfred A. Knopf, Inc.

RUN, RUN, AS
FAST AS YOU CAN

Mary Pope Osborne

236

Artist: MICHAEL DEAS
Art Director: Atha Tehon
Publisher: The Dial Press

237

Artist: MICHAEL DEAS
Art Director: Barbara Bertoli
Publisher: Avon Books

238
Artist: MICHAEL DEAS
Art Director: Bruce Hall
Publisher: Dell Books

239
Artist: JERRY PINKNEY
Art Director: Tom von Der Linn
Publisher: Reader's Digest

Artist: STEVE ASSEL   Art Director: Len Leone   Publisher: Bantam Books

Assel
'81

BIRDS, BEASTS AND
THE THIRD THING

POEMS BY D.H. LAWRENCE

241

Artist: ALICE and MARTIN PROVENSEN   Art Director: Barbara G. Hennessy   Publisher: Viking Penguin, Inc.

242

Artist: TOM HALL   Art Director: William Gregory   Publisher: Reader's Digest

243

Artist: SUSAN STILLMAN
Art Director: Earl Tidwell
Publisher: Book of The Month Club

JURY

DAVID K. STONE, Chairman
Freelance illustrator. Past President, Society of Illustrators.
Represented in Smithsonian Institute, Princeton University,
Aerospace Hall of Fame.

ROBERT ANTHONY
Graphic designer. President, Robert Anthony, Inc. Awards from ADC,
AIGA, SI, TDC.

WALTER BERNARD
Graphic designer/consultant to a variety of magazines. Taught at
Cooper Union. Board of Directors, AIGA.

NAIAD EINSEL
Illustrator/designer.

JOHN HUEHNEGARTH
Freelance illustrator.

ROGER HUYSSEN
Freelance illustrator.

B. MARTIN PEDERSEN
Graphic designer/teacher/lecturer. Senior partner, Jonson Pedersen
Hinrichs & Shakery. Board member, AIGA. Winner of many design
awards.

WALTER RANE
Freelance illustrator.

HOWARD ROGERS
Freelance illustrator/painter. Exhibits in galleries and museums
nationally.

ADVERTISING

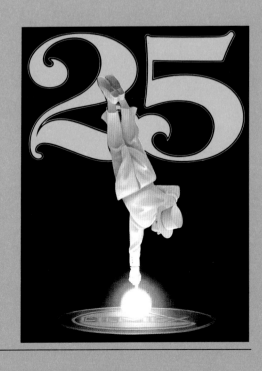

244

Artist: WILSON McLEAN
Art Director: Izumiya
Agency: Hakuhodo, Inc.
Client: Komatsu

GOLD MEDAL

245

Artist: SKIP LIEPKE
Art Director: Denise Minobe
Client: Elektra/Asylum/Nonesuch Records

GOLD MEDAL

246

Artist: ROBERT M. CUNNINGHAM
Art Director: Claudia Mengel
Client: Manufacturers Hanover Trust

SILVER MEDAL

247

Artist: CHARLES REID
Art Director: Ron Coro/Denise Minobe
Client: Elektra/Asylum/Nonesuch Records

SILVER MEDAL

248

Artist: JOHN COLLIER
Art Director: Henrietta Condak
Client: CBS Records

SILVER MEDAL

249
Artist: GERRY GERSTEN
Art Director: Martine Beudert
Agency: Lord, Geller, Federico, Einstein
Client: Quality Paperbacks

250
Artist: MARK HESS
Art Director: Bob Defrin
Client: Atlantic Records

251
Artist: ARTHUR LIDOV
Art Director: Burton Pollack
Client: Boehringer Ingelheim Ltd.

252
Artist: THOMAS BLACKSHEAR
Art Director: Jim Potter
Client: Lee Company

THE CANDLE SHOPPE

Artist: MARK TRACEY   Art Director: Mark Tracey   Client: Candle Shoppe

Artist: MARK ENGLISH   Art Director: Candy Santucci   Client: Eddie Bauer

255

Artist: BRUCE EMMETT
Art Director: Keith Munroe/Buffy Birritella
Client: Chaps/Ralph Lauren

256

Artist: DANIEL SCHWARTZ
Art Director: Ron Coro/Norm Ung
Client: Elektra/Asylum/Nonesuch Records

257

Artist: MARTIN GELLER
Art Director: Martin Geller
Client: The Kennedy Center for Performing Arts

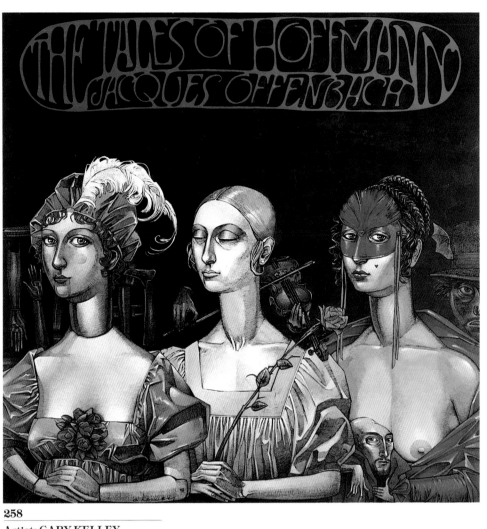

THE TALES OF HOFMANN
JACQUES OFFENBACH

258

Artist: GARY KELLEY
Art Director: Gary Kelley
Client: Iowa Center for The Arts

259

Artist: TED WRIGHT
Art Director: Ted Wright
Client: New York City Ballet Company

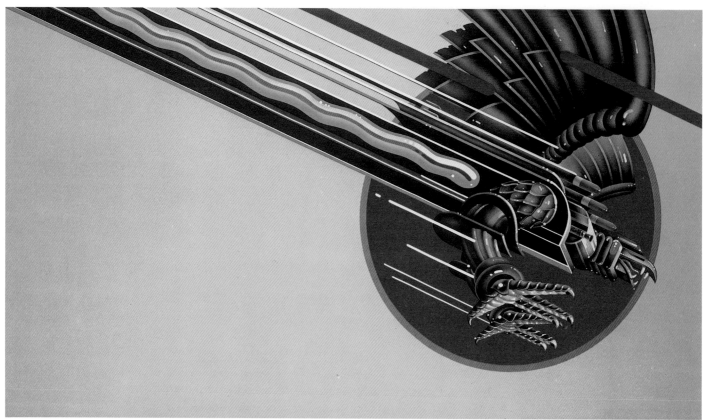

260
Artist: DOUG JOHNSON
Art Director: John Berg
Client: CBS Records

261
Artist: WILSON McLEAN
Art Director: Keith Bright/Bob Dion
Agency: Chiat/Day Advertising
Client: Holland American Cruise Lines

262
Artist: KEN DAVIES
Art Director: Irwin Goldberg
Agency: Nadler & Larimer, Inc.
Client: Austin, Nichols & Co., Inc.

263
Artist: TERESA FASOLINO
Art Director: Milton Glaser
Client: Grand Union

TULSA

Artist: PATTI FLEMING   Art Director: Ron Fleming   Agency: Graphic Associates   Client: City of Tulsa

265
Artist: DEBBIE WEEKLY
Art Director: Debbie Weekly
Agency: New West Group, Inc.
Client: McNeeley's Restaurant

266
Artist: JACQUELINE JASPER
Art Director: Ron Becker
Agency: Anesh, Viseltear, Gumbiner
Client: Kaiser Roth

267

Artist: KAREN KLUGLEIN

268
Artist: PEGGE HOPPER
Art Director: Jack O'Grady
Client: Jack O'Grady Galleries

269
Artist: DENNIS LUZAK
Art Director: Robert Durling
Agency: Ruvane•Leverte
Client: Surgikos

270

Artist: BART FORBES
Art Director: Anne Masters
Client: Time-Life Books

271

Artist: BILL CHAMBERS

272
Artist: CHARLES REID
Art Director: Ron Coro
Client: Elektra/Asylum/Nonesuch Records

273

Artist: TOMIE de PAOLA
Art Director: Diana Chase
Client: Neiman-Marcus

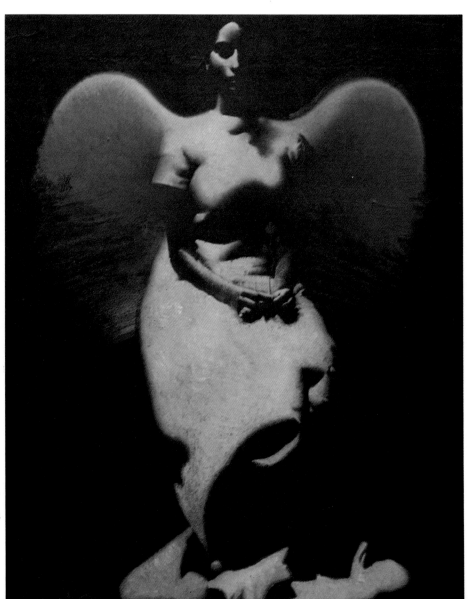

274

Artist: MARK ENGLISH
Art Director: Bart Forbes
Client: Vineyard Gallery

Artist: **BILL SELBY**   Art Director: Bill Selby   Client: Factors Etc., Inc.

276
Artist: FRED OTNES
Art Director: Gordon Fisher
Client: Neenah Paper

277
Artist: PAUL CRIFO
Art Director: Wayne Salo
Agency: Diener/Hauser/Bates
Client: Paramount

278
Artist: RICHARD SPARKS
Art Director: Sherry Pollack
Agency: McCaffrey & McCall
Client: Exxon PBS

279

Artist: STEVE KARCHIN
Art Director: Ko Noda
Client: Strathmore Paper Co.

280

Artist: **MARSHALL ARISMAN**
Art Director: Ron Coro/Denise Minobe
Client: Elektra/Asylum/Nonesuch Records

281

Artist: SEYMOUR CHWAST
Art Director: Paula Scher
Client: CBS Records

282
Artist: BRALDT BRALDS
Art Director: Nancy Rice
Agency: Fallon-McElligott-Rice
Client: Armour & Jack Frost Farms

283
Artist: BRALDT BRALDS
Art Director: Ton Giesbergen
Agency: TBWA Advertising
Client: Henkes Senefelder Printing House

284
Artist: GARY KELLEY
Art Director: Gary Kelley
Client: Western Michigan
University Theatre

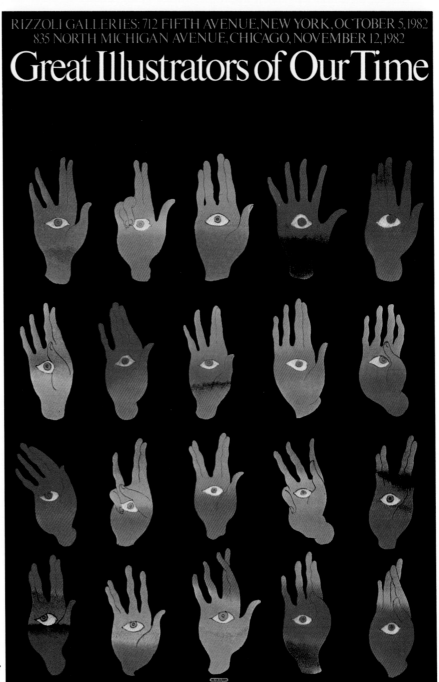

285
Artist: MILTON GLASER
Art Director: Milton Glaser
Client: Rizzoli Corporation

286
Artist: JACK ENDEWELT

287

Artist: DOUG JOHNSON
Client: Doug Johnson

288
Artist: MICHAEL GARLAND
Art Director: Denise Kronin
Client: Pantheon Books Promotion

289
Artist: DAVID GROVE
Art Director: Roy Alexander
Client: Walt Disney Productions

290
Artist: ATTILA HEJJA
Art Director: Joe Sonnaland
Agency: Mandabach & Simms
Client: Loral Electronic Systems

Artist: BRYAN HONKAWA
Art Director: Bryan Honkawa
Client: Wrather Port Properties

291
Artist: ATTILA HEJJA
Art Director: Joe Sonnaland
Agency: Mandabach & Simms
Client: Loral Electronic Systems

294
Artist: ELLEN RIXFORD
Art Director: Jane Trahey
Agency: Jane Trahey Associates
Client: Alexander Grant

295
Artist: MARY BURZYNSKI McMAHON
Art Director: Brian Nimeth
Agency: Griswold-Eshleman Co.
Client: Penton-IPC/Machine Design

293
Artist: DAVID BECK

296 & 297

Artist: ANTONIO LOPEZ   Art Director: John C. Jay   Client: Bloomingdale's

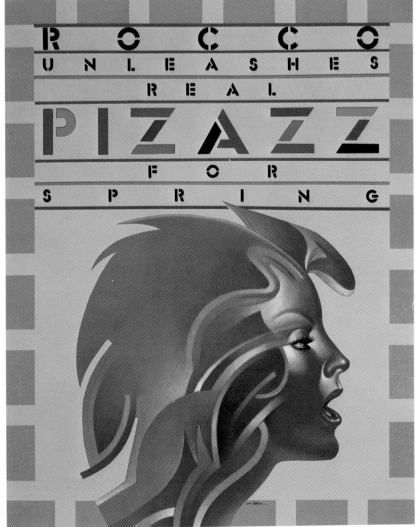

ROCCO UNLEASHES REAL PIZAZZ FOR SPRING

298

Artist: KIM BEHM
Art Director: Kim Behm
Client: Rocco Altobelli, Inc.

301

Artist: LARRY WINBORG   Art Director: Michael Mabry   Client: Watersmark

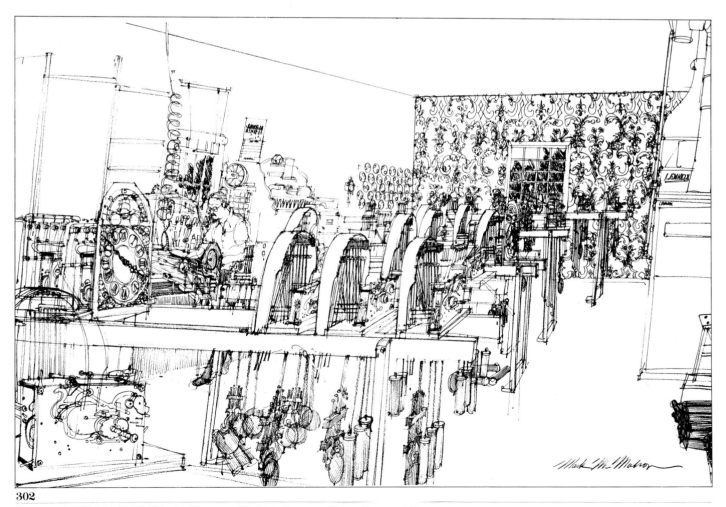

302

Artist: MARK M. McMAHON   Art Director: M.J. McGregor   Client: Kuempel Chime

303
Artist: NICHOLAS GAETANO
Client: Yochum-Kay

304
Artist: MARVIN MATTELSON
Art Director: Silas Rhodes
Client: School of Visual Arts

305
Artist: MILTON GLASER
Art Director: Milton Glaser
Client: San Diego Jazz Festival

306
Artist: MICHAEL SCHWAB

307
Artist: JACQUELINE
JASPER
Art Director: Larry Jennings
Client: Bergdorf Goodman

308
Artist: JACQUELINE JASPER
Art Director: Larry Jennings
Client: Bergdorf Goodman

309

Artist: TOM NACHREINER
Art Director: Tom Nachreiner
Client: Schlitz

310

Artist: JERRY PINKNEY
Art Director: Dave Foot/Terry McCaffrey
Client: U.S. Postal Service

311

Artist: RICHARD WALDREP   Art Director: Hannah Mayer   Agency: Richardson, Myers & Donofrio   Client: U.S.F. & G.

313
Artist: MILT KOBAYASHI
Art Director: Robert Durling
Agency: Ruvane•Leverte
Client: Surgikos

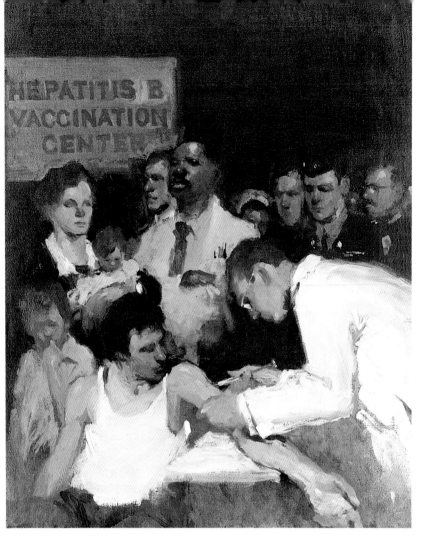

314
Artist: DICKRAN PALULIAN
Art Director: John Trentalange
Client: Roche Laboratories

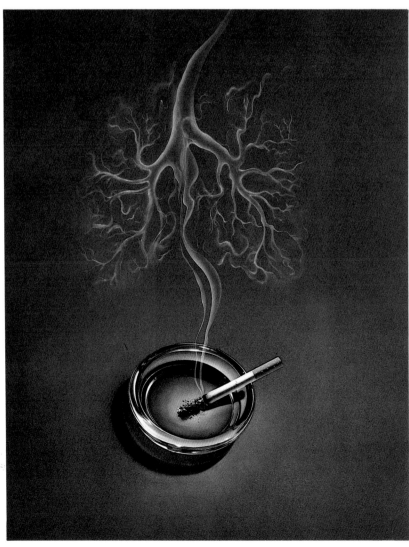

312
Artist: RICHARD MacDONALD
Art Director: Paul Selwyn
Agency: Keiler Advertising
Client: Avco International Enterprises

315
Artist: DEB MAHALANOBIS
Art Director: Paula Scher
Client: CBS Records

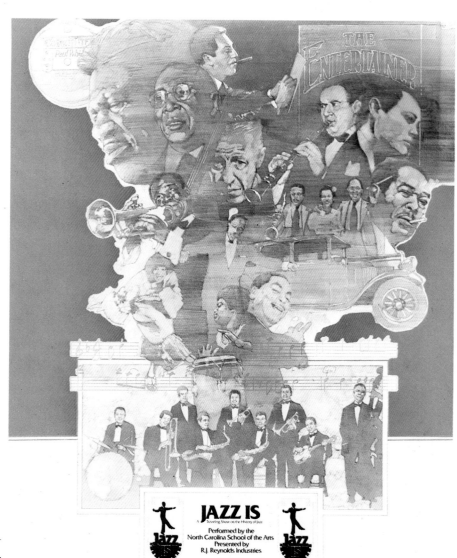

316

Artist: TIM BRUCE
Art Director: Linda Darnall
Client: R.J. Reynolds, Inc.

317

Artist: JERRY McDONALD
Art Director: Tony Lane
Client: CBS Records

318
Artist: NICHOLAS GAETANO
Client: GEO

319

Artist: ROBERT GIUSTI
Art Director: Allen Weinberg
Client: CBS Records

320
Artist: LORETTA LUSTIG

321
Artist: THEA KLIROS
Art Director: Victor Liebert/Ina Kahn
Client: Trevira

322
Artist: DARRYLIN LORD

PERRY ELLIS
1 9 8 2

323
Artist: BILL MAYER
Art Director: Bill Sweney
Agency: Cole Henderson Drake
Client: The French Restaurant

324
Artist: DREW STRUZAN
Art Director: Steve Bernstein
Agency: McCaffrey & McCall
Client: ABC Television Network

325
Artist: DREW STRUZAN
Art Director: Steve Bernstein
Agency: McCaffrey & McCall
Client: ABC Television Network

326

Artist: THOMAS BLACKSHEAR   Art Director: Jack Thorwegen   Agency: The Waylon Company   Client: Anheuser-Busch

327
Artist: NANCY FREEMAN
Art Director: Jim Temple
Agency: Ayer/Pritkin-Gibbon
Client: Granny Goose

328
Artist: LARRY WINBORG
Art Director: Michael Mabry
Client: Watersmark

329
Artist: RICHARD HUCK

330
Artist: MILTON GLASER
Client: Atlantic Deluxe

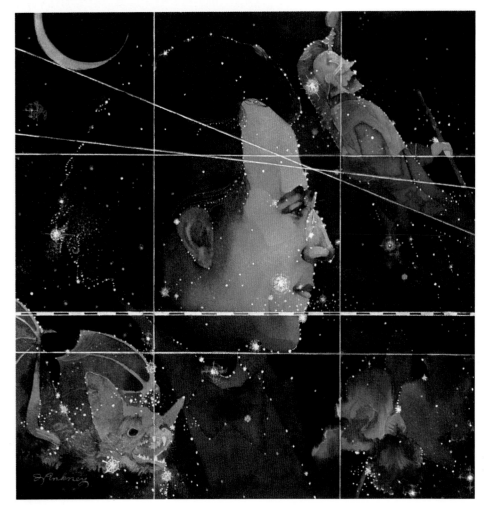

331
Artist: JERRY PINKNEY
Art Director: Joe Stelmach
Client: RCA Records

332

Artist: RICHARD MANTEL
Art Director: Ron Coro
Client: Elektra/Asylum/Nonesuch Records

We put a little heart
in everything we do.

Work thou for pleasure
paint, or sing, or carve
The thing thou lovest,
though the body starve...
Who works for glory misses
oft the goal;
Who works for money coins
his very soul.
Work for the work's sake,
then, and it may be
That these things shall be
added unto thee.
Kenyon Cox 1856—1919

Jann Church Advertising
& Graphic Design, Inc.
220 Newport Center Drive
Design Plaza
Newport Beach,
California 92660
Telephone 714/640-6224

Corporate Communications
Market Research
Identity Planning
Advertising
Corporate Public Relations
Marketing Brochures
Annual Reports
Environmental Signage Systems
Product Positioning
Package Design
Point of Purchase
Direct Mail

Design Jann Church Advertising & Graphic Design, Inc.   Lithography: IPD Printing & Distributing, Inc.   Typography: Andresen Typographics   Illustration: Lita Perone

Artist: ELWOOD SMITH   Art Director: Paula Scher   Client: CBS Records

335
Artist: STANISLAW ZAGORSKI
Art Director: John Channell
Client: Maxell Corporation of America

333
Artist: LEA PASCOE
Art Director: Jann Church/Lea Pascoe
Client: Jann Church Advertising & Graphic Design, Inc.

336
Artist: SKIP LIEPKE

337
Artist: ROBERT KUESTER
Art Director: Ray Brown/Larry McMurtry
Agency: Ross Roy Advertising
Client: United Negro College Fund

338
Artist: BERNIE FUCHS
Art Director: Don Krause
Agency: O'Grady Advertising Arts
Client: Jack Levy & Associates, Inc.

339

Artist: MAURICE LEWIS
Art Director: Bill White
Client: Rains Tool Company

340
Artist: JOHN M. THOMPSON
Art Director: Bob Reedy
Agency: Needham, Harper & Steers
Client: Busch Beer

341
Artist: BART FORBES
Art Director: Elaine Lance
Client: Sanger-Harris

342
Artist: CAROL FORTUNATO
Art Director: Bob Heimall
Client: Accord Records

343
Artist: BOB CROFUT

344

Artist: GILBERT STONE   Art Director: Bob Defrin   Client: Atco Records

345
Artist: ANDY ZITO
Art Director: Nancy Donald
Client: CBS Records

346
Artist: GREG WINTERS

347
Artist: ROGER HUYSSEN   Art Director: John Berg   Client: CBS Records

348
Artist: PETER M. FIORE
Art Director: Doug Fisher
Agency: Lord Sullivan Yoder
Client: Allen-A.

349
Artist: PETER M. FIORE
Art Director: Doug Fisher
Agency: Lord Sullivan Yoder
Client: Allen-A.

350
Artist: PETER M. FIORE
Art Director: Doug Fisher
Agency: Lord Sullivan Yoder
Client: Allen-A.

351

Artist: BRAD HOLLAND
Art Director: Brad Holland/Harlan Quist
Client: The American Book Awards

352
Artist: WILSON McLEAN   **Art Director:** Keith Bright/Bob Dion   **Agency:** Chiat/Day, Advertising   **Client:** Holland American Cruise Lines

353
Artist: **NICHOLAS GAETANO**   Client: **Mirage Editions**

354

Artist: BERNIE FUCHS   Art Director: Sam Cooperstein   Agency: Benton & Bowles   Client: A.M.F.

355

Artist: **WILSON McLEAN** Art Director: Keith Bright/Bob Dion Agency: Chiat/Day, Advertising Client: Holland American Cruise Lines

356
Artist: PAUL R. ALEXANDER
Art Director: James Adair
Agency: Geer-Dubois, Inc.
Client: International
Business Machines

357
Artist: CHARLES SANTORE
Art Director: Elmer Pizzi
Agency: Grey & Rogers
Client: Diamond Shamrock

359
Artist: JÖZEF SUMICHRAST
Art Director: Dobbi Massey
Agency: Klemtner Advertising, Inc.
Client: USV Laboratories

360
Artist: JÖZEF SUMICHRAST
Art Director: Dobbi Massey
Agency: Klemtner Advertising, Inc.
Client: USV Laboratories

361
Artist: CHUCK PYLE
Art Director: Greg McVey
Client: GEMCO/Lucky Stars

362
Artist: MEL FURUKAWA
Art Director: Peter Farago
Agency: Geer-Dubois, Inc.
Client: Ina Corporation

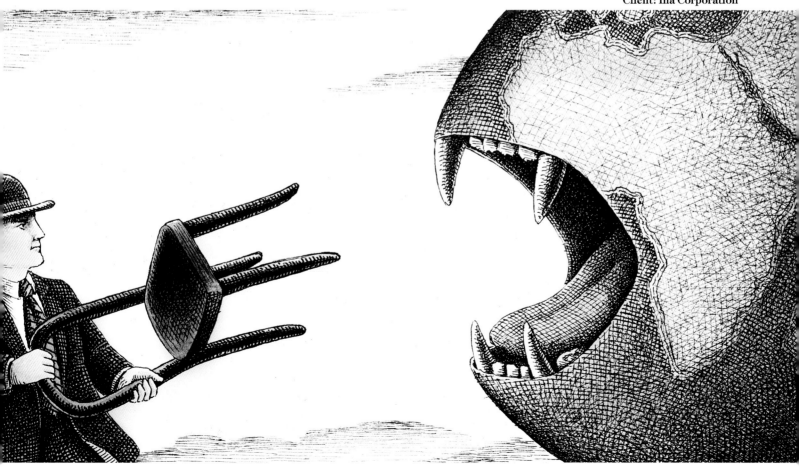

363

Artist: JIM SHARPE   Art Director: Jim Sharpe   Client: Frank Goodman Associates

Mobil Showcase Network   Charles Dickens' The Life and Adventures of

NICHOLAS NICKLEBY

THE ROYAL SHAKESPEARE COMPANY'S PRODUCTION   A NINE HOUR SERIES ON FOUR CONSECUTIVE TUESDAYS
HOST: PETER USTINOV   JANUARY 10 11 12 13   8 PM

Artist: SEYMOUR CHWAST   Art Director: Sandra Ruch   Client: Mobil Oil Corporation

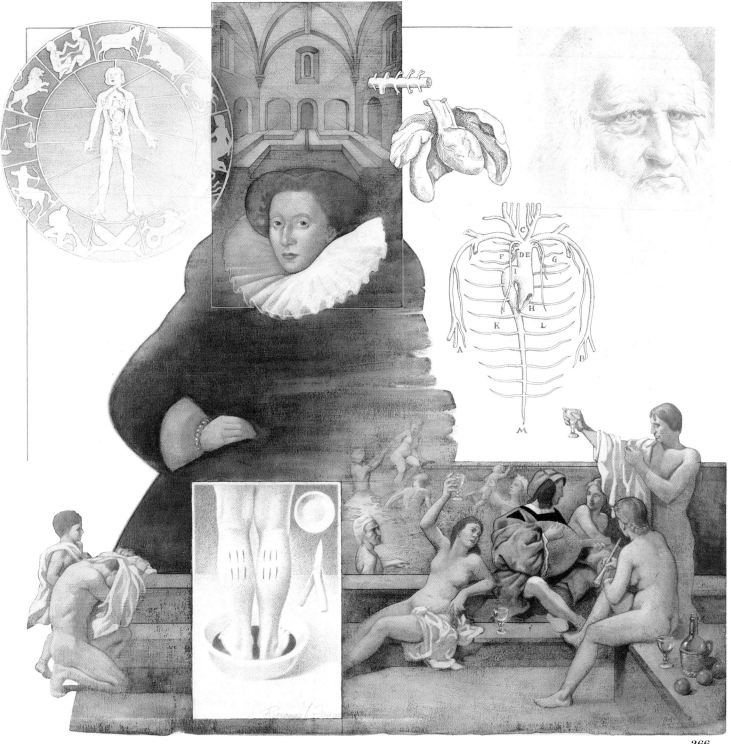

366
Artist: RAY SRUGIS
Art Director: Cathy de Martin
Agency: Ruvane•Leverte
Client: Organon Pharmaceuticals

365
Artist: MARK HESS
Art Director: Gary Alfredson
Agency: Ketchum, MacLeod, Grove
Client: Pennsylvania Tourist Office

JURY

JOHN WITT, Chairman
Illustrator/portraitist. Past President, Society of Illustrators.
Represented in U.S. Navy and Air Force art collections.

CHRISTOPHER BLOSSOM
Freelance illustrator. Son and grandson of illustrators. Exhibits marine
paintings nationally.

BRALDT BRALDS
Freelance illustrator/designer. Awards from CA Magazine, N.Y. and L.A.
Society of Illustrators.

LINDA CROCKETT
Freelance illustrator. SI Annual Exhibition award winner. Exhibits U.S.
and abroad.

GENE FEDERICO
Art director. Founder of Lord, Geller, Federico, Einstein, Inc.
ADC, AIGA, TDC award winner. ADC Hall of Fame, 1980.

SANFORD KOSSIN
Freelance illustrator. SI Annual Exhibition award winner.

JACKIE MERRI MEYER
Art Director, Macmillan Publishing Company. Awards from ADC,
Advertising Club.

KEITH REYNOLDS
Painter/designer. President, Mystic River Studios. Consultant for
Colonial Williamsburg, Smithsonian Institute, Hayden Planetarium.

JEFF SEAVER
Freelance illustrator. National Vice-President, Graphic Artists Guild.

INSTITUTIONAL

367   Artist: GARY KELLEY   Art Director: Gary Kelley   Client: University of Iowa Dance Program   **GOLD MEDAL**

368   Artist: BILL NELSON   Art Director: Bill Nelson   Client: The Poster Gallery   **SILVER MEDAL**

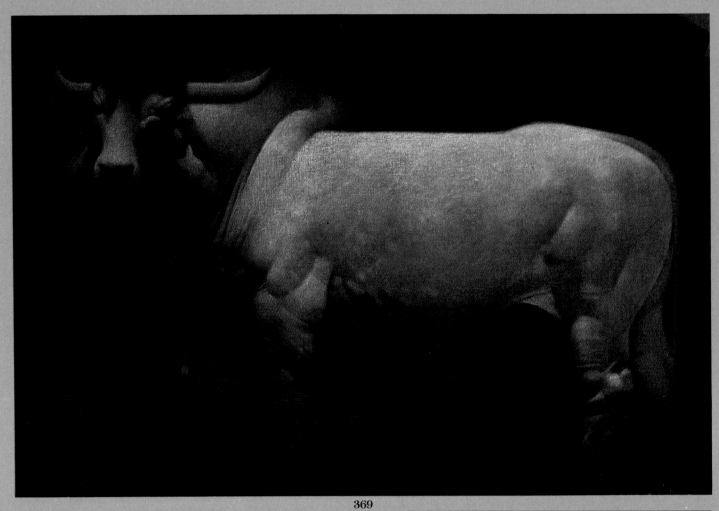

369

Artist: MARK ENGLISH
Art Director: Jack O'Grady
Client: Jack O'Grady Galleries

SILVER MEDAL

370   **Artist: MARK ENGLISH   Art Director: Jack O'Grady   Client: Jack O'Grady Galleries   SILVER MEDAL**

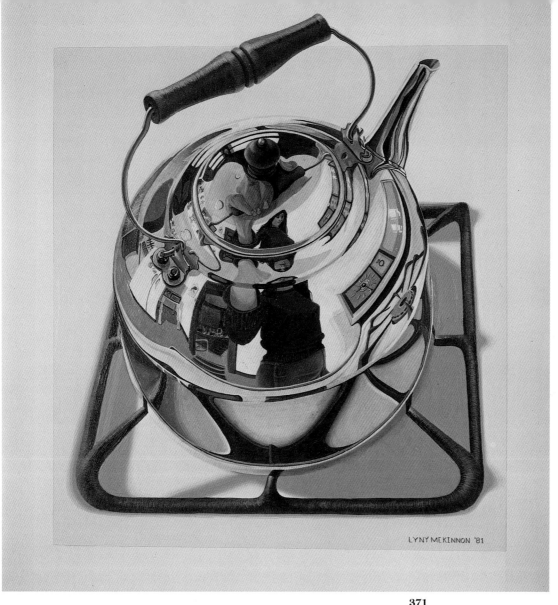

371
Artist: LYN D.S. McKINNON

372
Artist: CAROLYN BRADY
Art Director: Bennett Robinson
Client: H.J. Heinz Company

373

Artist: DAVID WILCOX   Art Director: Bennett Robinson   Client: H.J. Heinz Company

374

Artist: BURT SILVERMAN
Art Director: Stefan Geisbuhler
Agency: Chermayeff & Geismar
Client: Edward S. Gordon Co.

375

Artist: NICK C. STAMAS
Art Director: Nick C. Stamas
Client: Merrell Dow Pharmaceuticals, Inc.

376
Artist: JAMES McMULLAN
Art Director: Bennett Robinson
Client: H.J. Heinz Company

377
Artist: ROBERT WEAVER
Art Director: Bennett Robinson
Client: H.J. Heinz Company

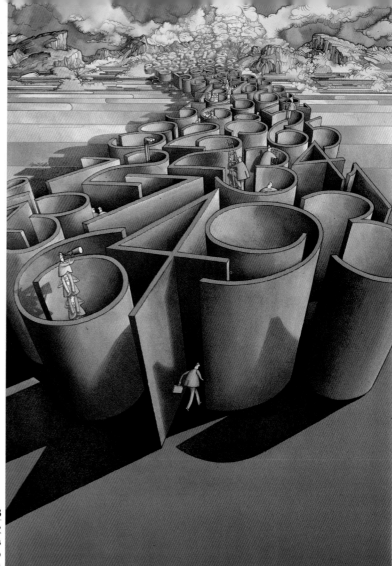

378
Artist: BENTE ADLER
Art Director: Jim Richards
Agency: Turner Richards Group
Client: Kaye Instruments

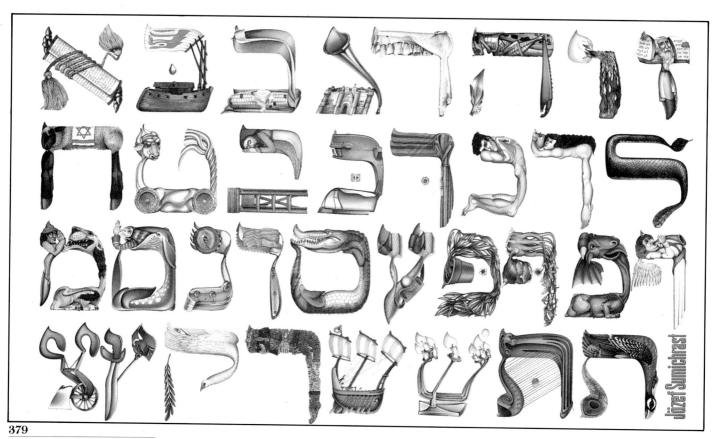

379

Artist: JÖZEF SUMICHRAST

Artist: RICHARD MANTEL   Art Director: Allan Peckolick   Client: Coopers & Lybrand

381

Artist: KAZUHIKO SANO

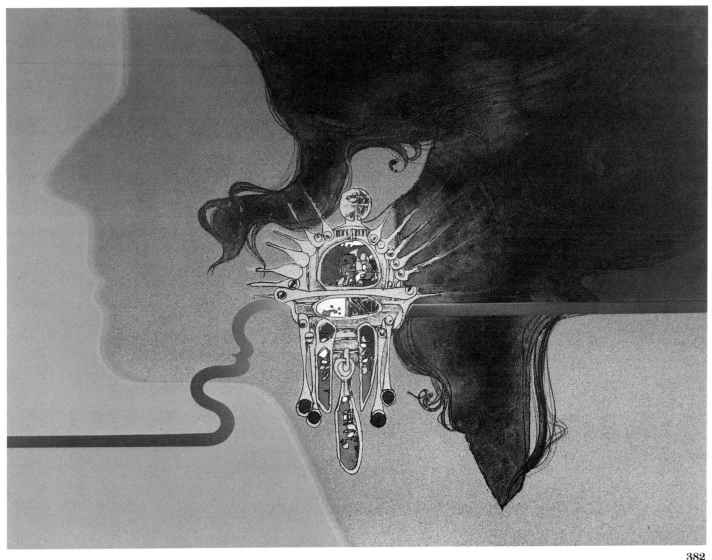

382

Artist: BOB PEAK
Art Director: Bob Peak
Client: Jack O'Grady Galleries

383

Artist: MIKE DURBIN
Art Director: Virginia & Lynn Bussey
Client: The Great Hang Up

384
Artist: THOMAS R. AUBREY

385
Artist: LISA FRENCH
Art Director: Kit Hinrichs
Client: Crocker Bank—Assets Magazine

386

Artist: JAMES McMULLAN

389

Artist: JOHN COLLIER   Art Director: Bennett Robinson   Client: H.J. Heinz Company

390
Artist: DAVIS HANNAH
Art Director: Bob Dacey
Client: Davis Hannah Illustration

391
Artist: MEREDITH NEMIROV

392
Artist: MICHAEL HALBERT   Client: Neenah Paper

393
Artist: NANCY LAWTON

394

Artist: GARY KELLEY

395
Artist: ALAN HASSINGER

396
Artist: FRED OTNES   Art Director: Dick Hess   Client: Champion Paper

397
Artist: SUDI McCOLLUM   Art Director: Sudi McCollum   Client: McCollum & Pitcher

398
Artist: DANIEL SCHWARTZ   Art Director: Neil Shakery   Client: AMFAC

399
Artist: WILSON McLEAN
Art Director: Bennett Robinson
Client: Eli Lilly & Company

400

Artist: PAMELA LEE

401
Artist: IZUMI INOUE

402
Artist: MATT MAHURIN

403

Artist: DAVID GRIFFIN   Art Director: Matthew Watson   Client: Matthew Watson

404

Artist: BERNIE FUCHS   Art Director: Jack O'Grady   Client: Jack O'Grady Galleries

405
Artist: TED COCONIS

407
Artist: MARK SKOLSKY

406
Artist: BOB ZIERING
Art Director: Bob Ziering
Client: Jerry Anton

408
Artist: BILL SIENKIEWICZ

Artist: JEFF SEAVER

410
Artist: ROBERT MORELLO

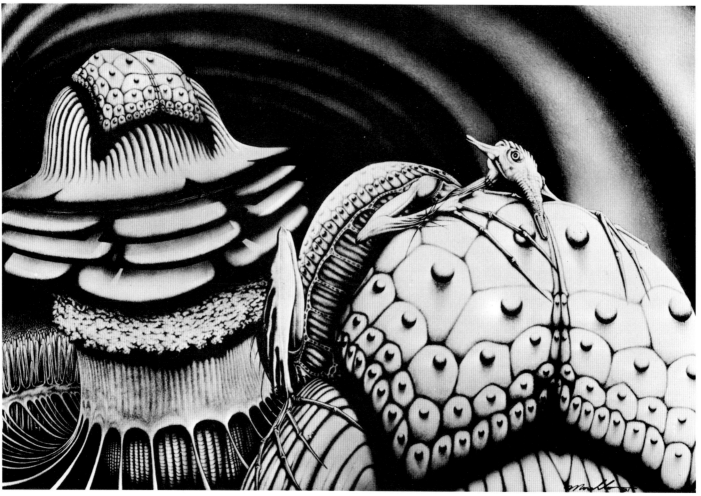

411

Artist: WILSON McLEAN
Client: Galerie Vontobel

412
Artist: RON THURSTON
Art Director: Tony Sikorski

413
Artist: KEITH FERRIS
Art Director: Keith Ferris
Client: Air Force Art Program

414
Artist: DOUG JOHNSON
Art Director: Joseph Papp
Client: The Public Theatre

415

Artist: MIRIAM SCHOTTLAND
Art Director: Robert Schulman
Client: NASA

Artist: ARTHUR and ALAN SINGER
Art Director: Howard Paine/Stevan Dohanos
Client: U.S. Postal Service

417

Artist: SUDI McCOLLUM
Art Director: Sudi McCollum
Client: Michael Patrick Cronan

418
Artist: JIM JONSON

419

Artist: ROBERT HEINDEL
Art Director: John deCesare
Client: Lindenmeyr Paper Corporation

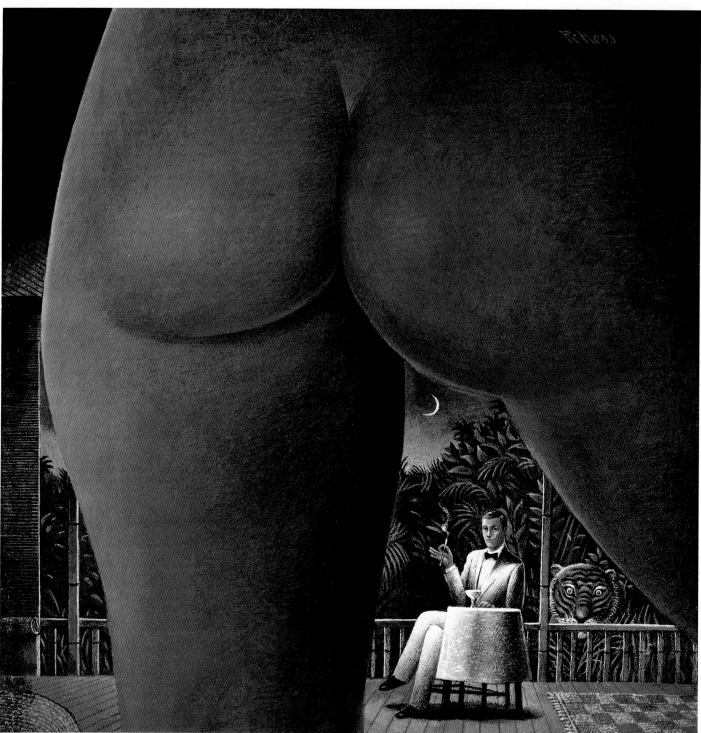

420
Artist: RICHARD HESS
Art Director: Shinichiro Tora/Yashharu Nakahara
Client: Hotel Barmen's Association

421
Artist: BOB PEAK
Art Director: Jack O'Grady
Client: Jack O'Grady Galleries

The SOPHISTICATED TRAVELER

422

Artist: MICHAEL DORET   Art Director: Andrew Kner   Client: The New York Times Travel Section

423
Artist: DENNIS ZIEMIENSKI

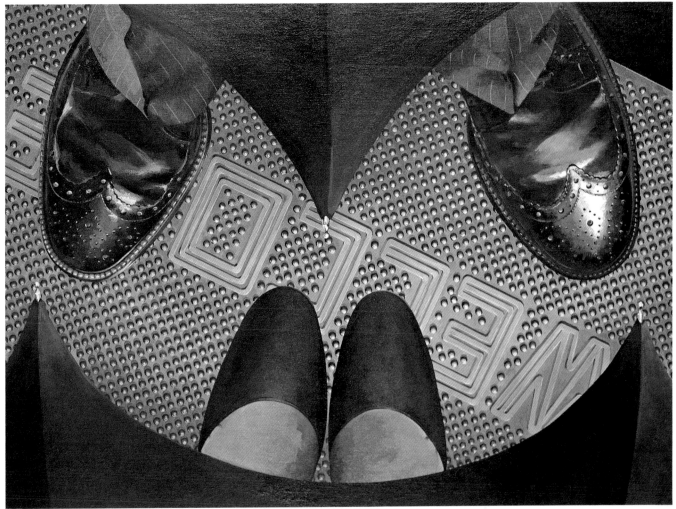

424
Artist: PAT DUFFY

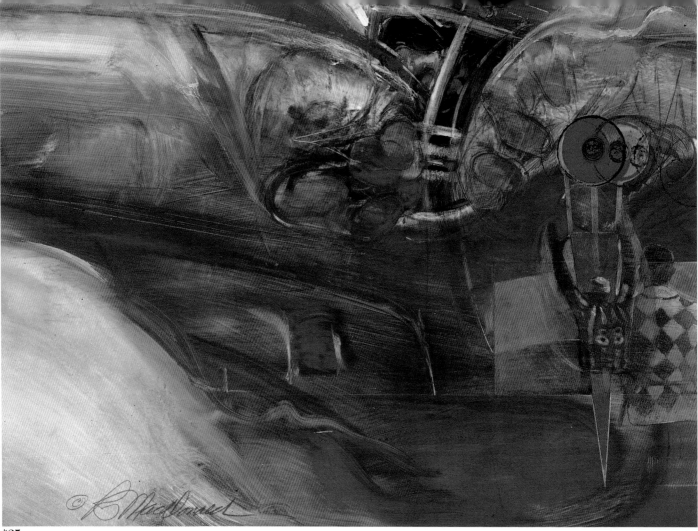

425
Artist: RICHARD MacDONALD
Art Director: Darrell Mayabb
Client: Pizza Hut

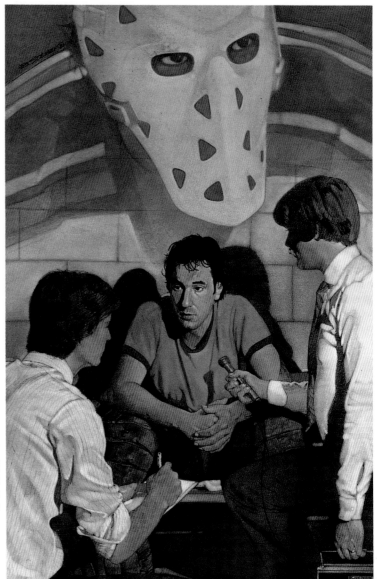

426
Artist: FRANK A. STEINER
Art Director: Susie Mathieu
Client: St. Louis Blues

427
Artist: MARK M. McMAHON
Art Director: Tom Conney
Client: Loyola University

428
Artist: GLENN BATKIN

429

Artist: LARRY GERBER   Art Director: Barbara Gerber

430

Artist: ANDY BUTTRAM

431

Artist: DAVID GROVE
Art Director: E. Carl Leick/Jim Kelly
Client: Western Airlines

432

Artist: WILLIAM V. CIGLIANO
Art Director: Jim Lienhart
Agency: Murrie, White, Drummond, Lienhart
Client: Bill Cigliano/Nancy Peck

433

Artist: RICHARD MacDONALD
Art Director: Bob Brandon/Rick Wemmers
Client: Anheuser-Busch

434

Artist: KRISTOPHER COPELAND
Art Director: Ron Swenson
Client: School of The Associated Arts

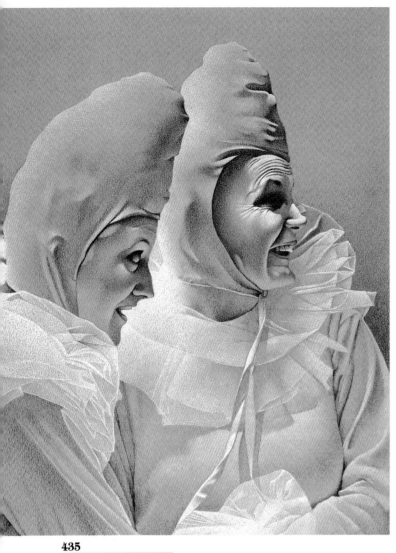

435
Artist: BILL NELSON

436
Artist: BILL NELSON
Art Director: Mark Goldstein
Client: National Public Radio

437
Artist: JAMES E. TENNISON
Art Director: James E. Tennison/Philip Hayes
Client: The Los Angeles International Film Exposition

Artist: JACK UNRUH
Art Director: Nancy Hoefig
Agency: Richards, Sullivan, Brock & Associates
Client: Lomas & Nettleton

440

Artist: JACK UNRUH
Art Director: Nancy Hoefig
Agency: Richards, Sullivan, Brock & Associates
Client: Lomas & Nettleton

438

Artist: RICHARD SPARKS
Art Director: Elton S. Robinson
Client: Exxon Corporation

441

Artist: BUD KEMPER   Art Director: Bud Kemper

442

Artist: HENRY KOLODZIEJ

443

Artist: RAUL DEL RIO
Art Director: Kirk Hinshaw
Agency: Dancer, Fitzgerald, Sample
Client: San Francisco Zoological Society

80 84

444
Artist: DAVID LESH   Art Director: Sara Love   Client: David Lesh

445

Artist: BART FORBES Art Director: Jack O'Grady Client: Jack O'Grady Galleries

446

Artist: ROBERT A. OLSON
Art Director: Robert A. Olson
Client: Windemere Galleries

447

Artist: CAROL WALD
Art Director: Jacqueline Dedell
Client: Jacqueline Dedell

448
Artist: WILLIAM LOW

450
Artist: JERI FROEHLICH/KEITH GODARD
Art Director: Keith Godard
Client: Municipal Art Society

449
Artist: WILLIAM LOW

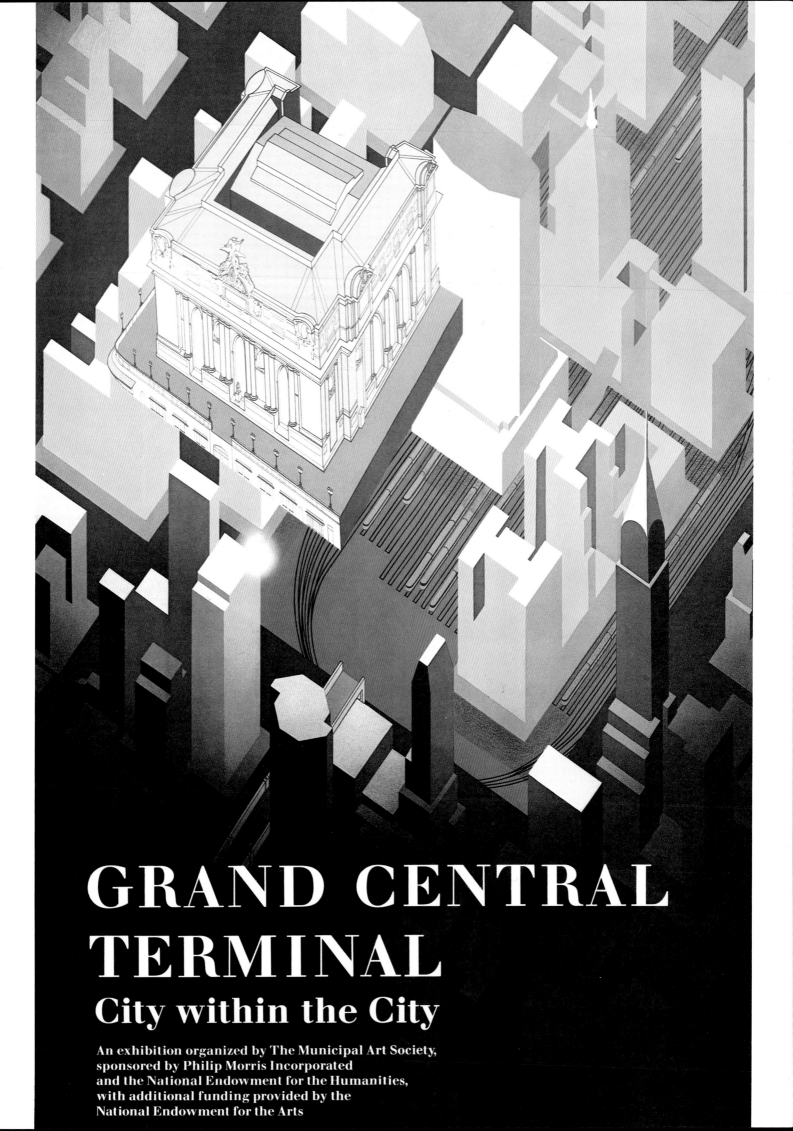

GRAND CENTRAL
TERMINAL
City within the City

An exhibition organized by The Municipal Art Society,
sponsored by Philip Morris Incorporated
and the National Endowment for the Humanities,
with additional funding provided by the
National Endowment for the Arts

Kawasaki

451

Artist: WAYNE WATFORD

455
Artist: DICK LUBEY
Art Director: Karen Bopp
Client: Alling & Cory Co.

456
Artist: CRAIG CALSBEEK
Art Director: Don Mennel
Client: Playboy Jazz Festival

457

Artist: **MILTON GLASER**
Art Director: Milton Glaser
Client: Whiteprint Editions

458

Artist: **EARL KELENY**

459

Artist: ROBERT HEINDEL
Art Director: Shinichiro Tora
Client: Hotel Barmen's Association

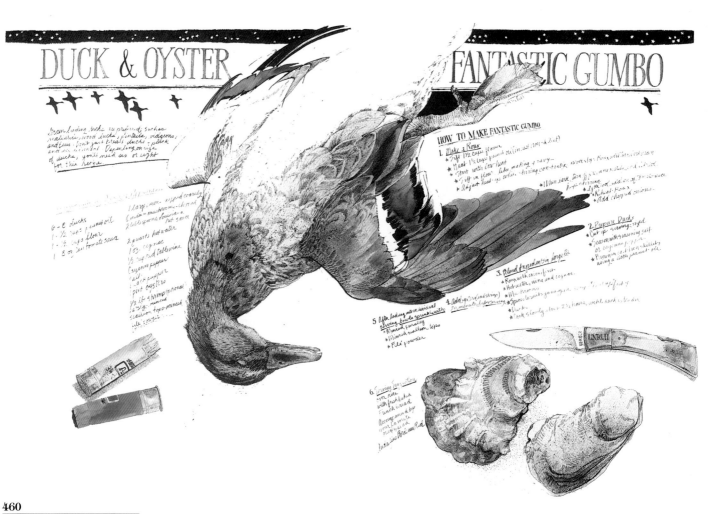

DUCK & OYSTER

FANTASTIC GUMBO

460
Artist: JACK UNRUH
Art Director: Mike Windsor
Client: American Press

461
Artist: ARTHUR and ALAN SINGER
Art Director: Howard Paine/Stevan Dohanos
Client: U.S. Postal Service

462
Artist: JEFFREY TERRESON

463

Artist: LOUIS ESCOBEDO
Art Director: Louis Escobedo
Client: Thompson Press

464

Artist: MURRAY TINKELMAN
Art Director: Shinichiro Tora
Client: Hotel Barmen's Association

465

Artist: J. RAFAL OLBINSKI   Art Director: J. Rafal Olbinski   Client: Old Warsaw Galleries, Inc.

466

Artist: WENDY BUSKEY   Art Director: Bill Cunningham   Client: Hallmark Cards, Inc.

467
Artist: GLENN HARRINGTON

468
Artist: HARRIET PERTCHIK

478
Artist: DAVID LESH
Art Director: Sara Love
Client: David Lesh

479

Artist: MAURICE LEWIS

480

Artist: DONALD GATES
Art Director: Claudia Burwell
Client: Ladycom

481

Artist: DOUG JOHNSON   Art Director: Cye Jacobson   Client: Burlington Industries

482

Artist: MARK M. McMAHON
Art Director: Carolyn M. Gregor
Client: Highland House Design

484
Artist: JIM BUCKELS
Art Director: Kelly Weaver
Client: Bonaroō Graphics

485
Artist: ALAN E. COBER
Art Director: John deCesare
Client: The Illustrators Workshop

486

Artist: **ROBERT GIUSTI**   Art Director: **Bennett Robinson**   Client: **H.J. Heinz Company**

487

Artist: JOYCE HAYASHI
Art Director: Don Dubowski
Client: Hallmark Cards, Inc.

Wolf Trap Lives, 1982

America's National Park For The Performing Arts

488
Artist: MILTON GLASER
Art Director: Milton Glaser
Client: United Technologies & Wolf Trap

489
Artist: BART FORBES

490
Artist: BOB PEPPER
Art Director: Jill Baker
Client: Sunrise Greeting Cards

491
Artist: KAZUHIKO SANO

492

Artist: WILLIAM A. SLOAN

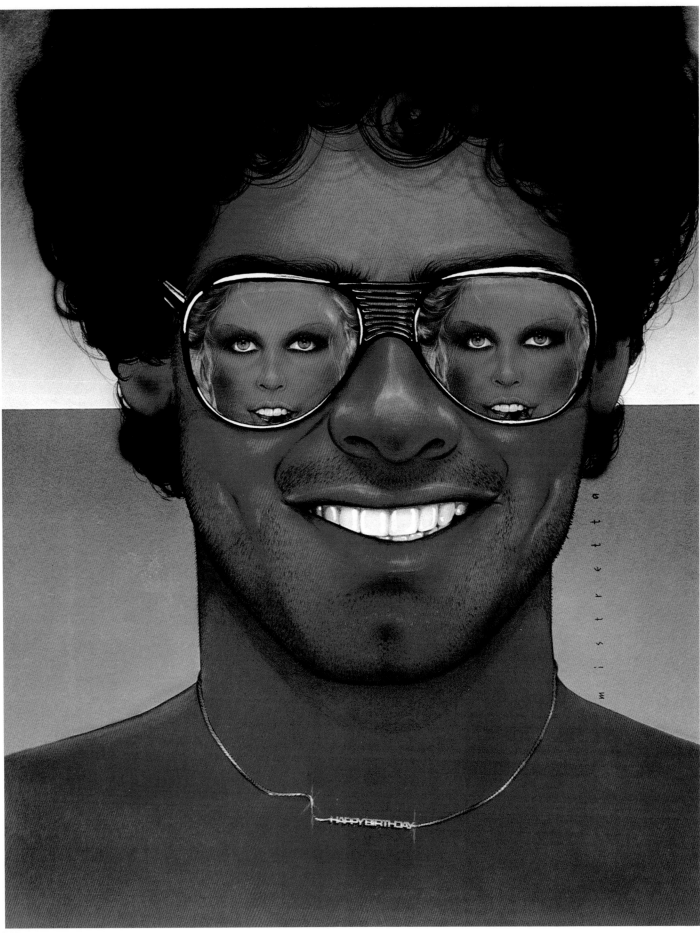

493

Artist: ANDREA MISTRETTA

494

Artist: BILL SIENKIEWICZ

495

Artist: BOB DORSEY

AMERICAN HORSE

496
Artist: MARK ENGLISH
Art Director: Brad Thompson
Client: U.S. Postal Service

497
Artist: ROBERT F. GOETZL

498
Artist: FRANCO ACCORNERO

TONY AGPOON DESIGN
410 TOWNSEND STREET, SUITE 408c
SAN FRANCISCO, CA. 94107
415 541 0523

© 1992 TONY AGPOON DESIGN   COPY: KARBELL NASUX

499

Artist: TONY AGPOON
Art Director: Tony Agpoon
Client: Tony Agpoon Design

500
Artist: DOUG PEARSON
Art Director: Jack O'Grady
Client: Jack O'Grady Galleries

501
Artist: MITCHELL ANTHONY

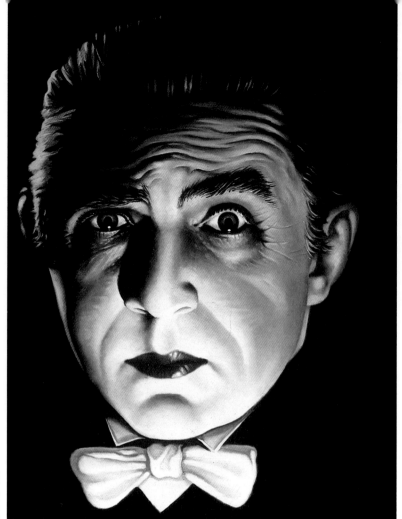

502
Artist: GARY RUDDELL
Art Director: Gary Ruddell
Client: Papermoon Graphics

503
Artist: TIMOTHY SCOGGINS

504

Artist: WAYNE WATFORD

505

Artist: BILL NELSON

506
Artist: CYNTHIA WATTS CLARK

507
Artist: JANET MAGER
Art Director: Gill Fishman
Client: Rainboworld

508
Artist: PAUL ORLANDO
Art Director: Dave King
Client: The 7 Up Company

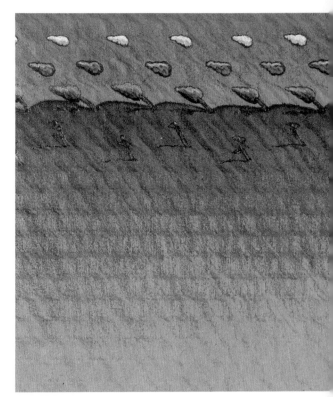

509
Artist: DICK MITCHELL
Art Director: Dick Mitchell
Agency: Richards, Sullivan, Brock & Associates
Client: Schroder Real Estate

Artist: JOHN M. CERNAK

Artist: PAUL ORLANDO
Art Director: Dave King
Client: The 7 Up Company

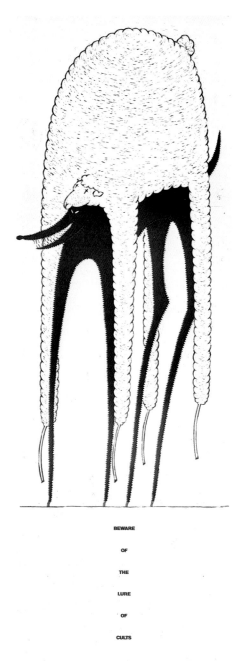

BEWARE

OF

THE

LURE

OF

CULTS

YPO

Child psychologist Dr. Sandy Andron speaks on the dangers of cults at the next meeting of the Dallas Chapter of YPO. Please join us Friday, January 15, at 6:30 p.m. in the auditorium of The Hockaday School (valet parking at the Welch Road entrance). Dinner will be served following the program. YPO'ers, qualified guests, and teenagers are invited to hear Dr. Andron clear up a lot of woolly thinking about cults and their followers.

Since he's be the evening are free and See Esther. Reply card enclosed.

512
Artist: CHRIS ROVILLO
Art Director: Chris Rovillo
Client: Young Presidents Organization

513
Artist: ROBERT A. OLSON
Art Director: Nancy Capetz
Client: Oasis Art Company

516
Artist: DICKRAN PALULIAN
Art Director: Robert Finch
Client: Papermoon Graphics

517
Artist: KEN TAYLOR
Art Director: Lillian Zamanian
Client: Art Staff Inc.

518

Artist: LARRY GERBER   Art Director: Barbara Gerber

519

Artist: LARRY GERBER   Art Director: Barbara Gerber

520
Artist: WILLIAM LOW

521

Artist: ROBERT M. CUNNINGHAM
Art Director: Bennett Robinson
Client: H.J. Heinz Company

522
Artist: JOHN P. SCHMELZER

523
Artist: MARTIN PATE

524
Artist: BOB PEAK

525
Artist: THOMAS KINKADE
Client: Biltmore Galleries

526

Artist: JUDY PEDERSEN

The Society of Illustrators Museum of American Illustration

The museum presented an exceptionally fine series of exhibitions during the past year. Besides the Annual Exhibition of the best editorial, book, advertising, and institutional illustration, the shows ran the gamut from the Cream of Wheat paintings of the '20's to the contemporary and controversial "New Illustration" show—as wide a spectrum of illustration as it is possible to present.

They were chosen with the intent of presenting the best of contemporary illustration and also presenting an historical background of illustration as an artform. Examples of the various exhibitions appear on the following pages.

Thanks and credit go to the Museum Committee: Robert Blattner, former president ADC and AD of Reader's Digest. Tom Cathey, Chairman of Hanging Committee. John Moodie, former president of SI and Chairman of Permanent Collection. Howard Munce*, former president SI, teacher and author of "Sounds from the Bullpen". Walt Reed*, authority and author of numerous books on illustration. Murray Tinkelman*, teacher and award winning illustrator. John Witt, former president SI and portrait painter. Art Weithas*, Chairman Museum Committee.

Tom Cathey, as Hanging Chairman, did a splendid job of overseeing the installation of the exhibitions. Terry Brown acted in his usual capacity as curator-collating, collecting and publicizing the various exhibitions.

*also members of the Board of Selection—New Britain Museum of American Art.

Left to right, standing: John Witt, Tom Cathey, Robert Blattner, Murray Tinkelman, John Moodie; Left to right, seated: Terry Brown, Art Weithas, Walt Reed; Missing: Howard Munce
Photo: Constance Witt

The New Illustration

Simms Taback had an idea. He felt there was a whole new element of illustration out there that was not being adequately represented in annual exhibitions or group shows around the country. He dubbed it the "New Illustration" and planned a national competition. His committee: Doug Johnson, Wilson McLean, Jim McMullan and Barbara Nessim selected a jury of 12 art directors and illustrators who chose 200 pieces to hang in "a luminous, tradition breaking exhibit." (Carol Stevens, *Print Magazine.*)

Graphis Magazine in Switzerland and *Idea Magazine* in Japan saw fit to do features on the show. And in *Art Direction*, Pete Finch said, "There was unabashed satire of life in the '80s; there was controlled disorder . . . , there was, to some 'anti-art,' which shrugged off the traditional values of harmony and beauty in illustration. And the show was a success."

If one looks at new work appearing in places as traditional as *Time* and *The New York Times*, one can see the truth in Carol Steven's statement: "The Society of Illustrators exhibit has undoubtedly given the "New Illustration" a healthy shove toward the mainstream."

It was a show that sparked controversy; opinions ran the gamut. Now you can judge for yourself.

APRIL GREIMAN/JAYME ODGES

RICHARD BERNSTEIN

The New Illustration

JIM HEIMANN

MICK HAGGERTY

LAURIE ROSENWALD

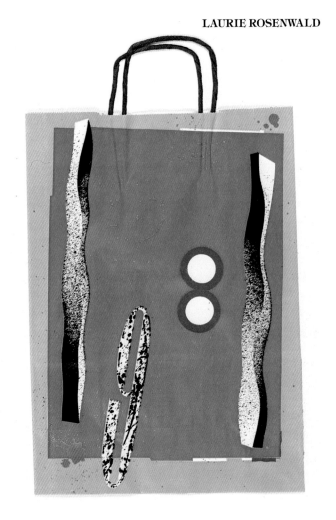

CYNTHIA MARSH

BOB ZOELL

NEON PARK

GARY PANTHER

PATER SATO

MONTXO ALGORA

LOU BROOKS

Exhibitions

JIM McMULLAN

"Revealing Illustrations" gave an insight into the creative process of New York illustrator Jim McMullan. He presented sketches, roughs and reference material which led to the finished work for such assignments as Brooklyn Discos (*New York Magazine*), Anna Christie (Liv Ullman's film) and December 25, 1914 (PBS Television). His works showed invention, craft, and thought and were received well by his contemporaries. Watson-Guptill's book, "Revealing Illustrations: The Art of James McMullan" was released concurrent with this exhibition's national tour.

"Anna Christie" Theatre Poster
©*Copyright James McMullan*

CREAM OF WHEAT

Robert M. Schaeberle, Chairman of the Board of Nabisco Brands Inc., was the Society's guest at the opening of the Cream of Wheat exhibition. The 40 original paintings for this All American product, many by Howard Pyle's students, were a smashing display of what is good in advertising art.

The video account of Cream of Wheat's successful advertising through art, "As good as you remember", accompanied the exhibition. Illustration giants, such as Flagg, Leyendecker, Sundblom and Loomis, were represented and are only a small part of Nabisco Brands Inc.'s impressive Cream of Wheat collection. Originals by Jessie Wilcox Smith, Katherine Wireman and Maude Tousey Fangel were also shown. This exhibition has toured nationwide through the efforts of Nabisco Brands Inc.'s archivist, Dave Stivers.

"He Thinks He's So Big" 1928, H.H. Sundblom
Courtesy of Nabisco Brands Inc.

"A Dainty Breakfast" 1909, J.C. Leyendecker
Courtesy of Nabisco Brands Inc.

Exhibitions

FRED FREEMAN

The U.S. submarine operations, the early days of the Polaris and Sealab programs and his work with Werner Von Braun at NASA are a few of the "New Frontiers" illustrated by Fred Freeman. The retrospective exhibition of his work presented these and other editorial illustrations. The display highlighted his draftsmanship, imagination and unique sense of composition. The underwater scene of an American P.O.W. striving to free himself from a sinking enemy submarine was an exceptionally dramatic illustration. The exhibition orginated at the Mystic Seaport Museum in Connecticut and traveled extensively.

"The Bubble" 1956 by Fred Freeman
casein on board 15 x 27
from the collection of Norman A. Turkish
©Copyright Fred Freeman 1982

MELBOURNE BRINDLE

Melbourne Brindle's retrospective exhibition put "magic realism" into sharp focus. His paintings of Rolls-Royce autos (1907-1914), rarely seen in the U.S., impressed many not only with his obvious love of the hardware but with the craft of his artistry. Done in the Trompe L'oeil tradition, they were strikingly simple yet had a personal spirit. Brindle's exhibition traced his early work on the West Coast (his San Francisco bridge series) to his current work in the Boston area (again painting bridges). *The Saturday Evening Post* and other editorial clients were represented. Brindle again positioned himself as a master of "magic realism."

Rolls-Royce "dickey seat" from "20 SILVER GHOSTS"
by Melbourne Brindle

WALT SPITZMILLER

"The Rodeo Painted" has become one of Walt Spitzmiller's best known series of paintings. The action-packed sport of rodeo has become his favorite subject. The exhibition of these and other selected works showed Spitzmiller's delicate wash style and his choice of luminescent colors. *Sports Illustrated* and other magazines were represented. Among the most striking images were his drawings of rodeo participants done with minimal line and maximum emotion.

"Sunlit Palomino" by Walt Spitzmiller
Courtesy Society of Illustrators Museum of American Illustration

HARVEY DUNN SCHOOL

"The Harvey Dunn School" proved to be the exhibition of most importance to the history of American illustration. Selected from private collections and the Society's Permanent Collection The Dunn Show presented great painting by Dunn and his students, including: Saul Tepper, Dean Cornwell, Mead Schaeffer, Lyman Anderson and Dan Content. Tepper's text enlivened the catalogue and presented a well focused view of "The Man, the Legend, and the School of Painting", which was Harvey Dunn. A display of World War One photos and books on Dunn added to the educational value of this show. It was enjoyed by the young and by many of Dunn's former students and seen by several art tour groups.

"Storming the Bastille" by Harvey Dunn
Courtesy the Society of Illustrators Museum of American Illustration

Harvey Dunn by Steven R. Kidd

"Stage Door—Schubert Theatre" by Saul Tepper
Courtesy the Society of Illustrators Museum of American Illustration

GOLDEN AGE OF COMICS

The idea of comic strip art being true art was projected in the exhibition "The Golden Age of Comics." Larry Bakke, Professor of Art at Syracuse University, wrote in the exhibition catalogue: "Nowhere in 20th Century Western illustrative form has the drawing and the text been so effectively fused as in the comics." The 129 works by 89 artists exhibited the best in humorous and adventure strips from 1900-1950. The public quickly recognized their favorites: Tarzan, The Little King, Flash Gordon, Bringing Up Father, Steve Canyon, Tippie and The Katzenjammer Kids, to name but a few.

"The Golden Age of Comics" was well attended; instructors and students discussing texture, older people recalling the strips they read as children, and young children seeing the Superman of 1942.

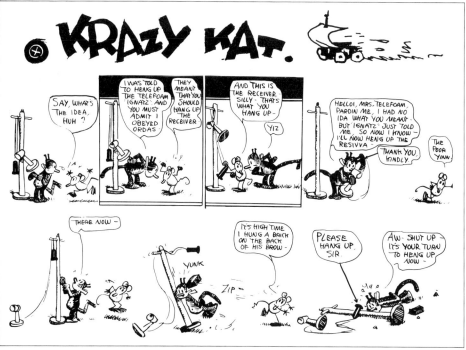

"Krazy Kat", George Herriman
Courtesy of Carol and Murray Tinkelman

Hamilton King Award Winners

"The Hamilton King Award Winners" exhibition featured illustrations by nineteen members of the S.I. This annual award is presented for "the best illustration of the year by a member of the Society." Recipients showed the award-winning original art and a second piece of their choosing. The list of artists who have won the Hamilton King Award reads like a who's who of contemporary American illustration. The first member to receive the honor was Paul Calle in 1965; 1983's winner is Robert M. Cunningham. The show attracted large, enthusiastic crowds. Lenders to this exhibition included: Joseph Mendola, Mr. and Mrs. Harold Gray, United Foods Inc., The U.S. Air Force Art Collection and The New Britain Museum of American Art.

1965 Paul Calle

1966 Bernie Fuchs

1969 Alan Cober

1970 Ray Ameijide

1971 Miriam Schottland

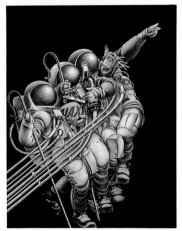

1972 Charles Santore

1973 Dave Blossom

1977 Leo & Diane Dillon

1978 Daniel Schwartz

1979 William Teason

1980 Wilson McLean

1981 Gerald McConnell

1982 Robert Heindel

Scholarship Exhibition

One of the major efforts by the Society of Illustrators to promote the art of illustration, is the annual student scholarship competition and exhibition. Limited to students at art schools, colleges and universities, the competition has drawn artwork from institutions located throughout the entire United States.

From modest beginnings over two decades ago, the annual scholarship competition has become the landmark exhibition for emerging young talent.

Each year from the thousands of entries submitted, approximately 180 pieces of art are selected by a jury of professional illustrators. Generous cash prizes are awarded, and each student represented in the exhibition is given a certificate of merit.

The selected artwork is displayed in the gallery of the Society's Museum of American Illustration, and affords the upcoming illustrator an unequaled showcase to present his work to the market place. In addition, a catalog showing reproductions of all the artwork in the exhibition, is ready for distribution upon the opening of the show.

We, at the Society of Illustrators, are proud indeed to afford the art world such a unique opportunity to become acquainted with the next generation of fine illustrators.

ALVIN J. PIMSLER
Chairman Education Committee

Garin Baker
Pratt Institute
David Passalacqua, Instructor
$1500 Lila Acheson Wallace Award
Top Right

Michael Christman
Art Center College of Design
Vince Robbins, Instructor
$1500 Society of Illustrators Award
Top Left

Vincent Nasta
School of Visual Arts
Jack Endewelt, Instructor
$1500 The Starr Foundation Award
Bottom Right

Designer: Bernie Karlin

Donors Luncheon, Society of Illustrators, April 29, 1983
seated Right to Left: John Witt, SI President; Gyo Fujikawa, Effie Bowie, Arch Unruh
and Linda Smith, Hallmark Cards, Inc., Robert H. Blattner, Warren Rogers.
Photo by: Arpi Ermoyan

New Acquisitions

It was a year of growth for the Permanent Collection. The Society was pleased to present three exhibitions of recent donations. Ten TIME MAGAZINE covers from the period 1943-1954 by Guy Rowe (GIRO) and the works donated by Lowell M. Schulman were seen in Gallery 3 (chairman, Mitchell Hooks). Mr. Schulman's gift included illustrations by Saul Tepper, Dean Cornwell, Peter Helck, F.C. Yohn and H.C. Edwards. 145 new acquisitions were shown in the Museum's two galleries in the Spring of 1982.

These represent a substantial increase in the quality and scope of the Society's Permanent Collection. Exhibitions in the Museum, loans to other exhibitions and travelling shows will draw upon this collection.

Much of the strength of the collection lies in the donations by contemporary artists. This year's donors included: Ken Bald, Melbourne Brindle, Judy Clifford, Steven R. Kidd, Howard Koslow, Robert Lavin, Robert McGinnis, Bob Pepper, Attilio Sinagra and Carol Wald.

Artwork was also donated by the families of the artists; gratitude is expressed to: Fritz Henning, Mark Mandel, Joanna B. Nielsen, Sheila Raleigh, Charles Rowe, Mrs. Noel B. Sickles, John M. Sykes and David & Lisa Tobler.

The Society also wishes to thank the following for their contributions of art to the Museum: Robert H. Blattner, Peter A. Brown, Mr. & Mrs. Terrence Brown, Charles Henry Carter, Mason Combs, Mr. & Mrs. Benjamin Eisenstat, Mr. & Mrs. Albert Gold, Dorothea Gramatky, Bruce & Elizabeth Hall, Illustration House, Daniel W. Keefe, Everett Raymond Kinstler, David Levine, George Loh, William J. Magner, Mrs. Harold C. Menger, John A. Moodie Jr., Elinor Farrell Murray, National Geographic Magazine, Russell F. Neale, Chuck Rowe, Lowell M. Schulman, Maurice Thomas and Janet & Arthur Weithas.

Gallery Three

The exhibition area on the third floor of the Society's headquarters is an attractive space for members to show new works. It is called Gallery Three and it has seen a remarkable cross section of the varied styles, techniques and media being employed by today's illustrators.

Subjects have ranged from anatomy to P.J. Clark's bar, from cartoon to realism. New Permanent Collection works and Hall of Fame Award Winners were also represented.

Some of the exhibiting artists were: Abby Merrill, Jeff Cornell, Jeanette Adams, Willis Pyle, Hal Ashmead, Harvey Kidder, D.L. Cramer, David K. Stone, Jill Karla Schwartz, John Schreck, Saul Mandel, Vic Valla, Barbara Carr.

The Society of Illustrators 1983-1984 Traveling Exhibition

In order to expand the audience which has seen and enjoyed the Society's exhibitions, a new program was undertaken this year. Six college level institutions will host a traveling show of 41 of America's top contemporary illustrators, including: Bernie Fuchs, Milton Glaser, Bob Peak, Alan E. Cober, Daniel Maffia, Mark English, Seymour Chwast, Brad Holland, Marshall Arisman and Doug Johnson. The public will be able to see a variety of media and approaches to a subject and with many accompanying tearsheets of the originals, they will be able to see the transition from painting to printed page.

This year long traveling show will be exhibited next summer at the Society of Illustrators Museum of American Illustration.

The six host schools are:

THE UNIVERSITY OF ALABAMA;
Tuscaloosa, Alabama
EAST CAROLINA UNIVERSITY;
Greenville, North Carolina
CONCORD COLLEGE;
Athens, West Virginia
KENDALL SCHOOL OF DESIGN;
Grand Rapids, Michigan
UNIVERSITY OF WISCONSIN;
Eau Claire, Wisconsin
KEYSTONE JUNIOR COLLEGE;
La Plume, Pennsylvania

Government Services

Each of the armed services of the United States maintains a collection of art telling the story of its part in the nation's history.

Since 1954 the Society of Illustrators has played a pivotal role in the ongoing creation of the Air Force Art Collection. Professional artists are selected from the membership and offered the opportunity to visit, witness and participate in specified Air Force missions and to record their impressions through art. The artist is free to choose his own subjects and to create the art he feels most appropriate for the collection.

Each artist travels and participates under invitational orders from the Secretary of the Air Force. In return for travel and expenses, the artists donates his time and talents and ownership of the artworks to the United States Government.

To facilitate administration and broaden the program, the Society of Illustrators of Los Angeles, the Society of Illustrators of San Francisco and the Artists Guild of Chicago have joined us in participation.

Almost 1000 artists have visited Air Force activities in the United States and throughout the world. The Air Force Art Collection now contains nearly 6000 works of art.

Reduced budgets of recent years have limited artist's travel when compared to earlier years. In spite of fewer trips, the Society of Illustrators contributed 48 works of art for the 1983 Air Force Art presentation.

These works were subject to a new Society of Illustrators policy and were juried by a panel of past Air Force Art Chairmen.

The Society of Illustrators is proud of the contribution of its membership to Air Force Art and is pleased to add our new association with the United States Coast Guard in a limited art program to document the Coast Guard mission.

P.A.L.

The Police Athletic League (PAL) sponsors an Art and Poetry contest for high school students. Since 1981 the Society has allocated funds to help these students embark on an art career. Each year PAL has provided matching funds and recently A.I. Friedman, Inc. has donated art supplies to the award winners. The Society sees this program as growing into a substantial scholarship fund.

Joint Ethics Committee

Since 1945, the Joint Ethics Committee has served the Graphic Industry by providing an alternative to litigation in the settlement of ethic disputes through peer review, mediation and arbitration.

Our six sponsors are the most respected professional organizations in the field: Society of Illustrators, The Art Directors Club, American Society of Magazine Photographers, Society of Photographers and Artist Representatives, Graphic Artist Guild, and the American Institute of Graphic Arts.

Selected representatives from these organizations serve as volunteers on the Committee. The services of the JEC are offered free of charge, and are available to anyone in the communications industry.

The J.E.C. has formulated a Code of Fair Practice which outlines the accepted ethical standards for the Graphics Industry. Send $2.50 for Code booklet or for further information please write to: Joint Ethics Committee, P.O. Box 179, Grand Central Station, New York, N.Y. 10163.

Art Weithas

Extremely versatile, Art Weithas has won awards in five different graphic categories: advertising, editorial, packaging, television and fine arts.

While he was art director at Elizabeth Arden, he designed the original dummy of Yank Magazine, then enlisted in the Army to become head art director of "Yank". He was awarded the Legion of Merit for his services as art director and combat artist-photographer in the Philippines (Corregidor, Zamboanga).

As original art director of Cover Girl cosmetics (SSC&B), he established its format and won awards in packaging and TV.

His concept of a book on combat art of the war evolved into his collaboration with James Jones on the classic, "WWII". He was the graphic director and designer.

He served as co-chairman of the Society of Illustrators exhibition, "200 Years of American Illustration", at the New-York Historical Society. This highly successful exhibition of over 950 illustrations broke all attendance records at the New-York Historical Society.

As chairman of the SI exhibition "20 Years of Award Winners", which presented all the award winners from the Society's Annual Exhibitions since 1960, he also designed a book with the same title. He edited Illustrators 24, the second annual produced entirely by the Society.

Art serves as Vice-President of the Society of Illustrators and Director of its Museum of American Illustration. He is also a Life Member of the NY Art Directors Club.

He is represented in the Army Center of Military History, Washington, D.C., the New Britain Museum of American Art where he serves on the Board of Selections, the SI Museum of American Illustration and COPAC, the Coast Guard Art Program.

A fine arts collector (Dufy, Pascin, Berman, Eric), he lives in New York City with his wife Janet.

Robert Anthony

Moderately versatile, Robert Anthony was born in Brooklyn, New York. He studied fine arts and graphic design on scholarships from the Art Students League, School of Visual Arts and Brooklyn Museum Art School. He now heads his own graphic design firm, Robert Anthony, Inc., founded in 1967, servicing clients in fields as varied as financial, restaurant-hotel, publishing and travel. His design and sales promotion background was established at Sudler and Hennessey, McCann Erickson (SCI) and Norman, Craig & Kummel (V.P., MPI). He is an active member of the Art Directors Club of New York, GAG, American Institute of Graphic Arts & Society of Illustrators. He has received numerous design awards including AIGA Communication Graphics, AIGA Cover Show, Creativity, Society of Illustrators, Print Case Books, Type Directors Club, Art Directors Club and others. His paintings have been exhibited in many group and one-man shows. He is a Grand Prix racing enthusiast and enjoys photographing motor racing, where he has occasionally been able to combine business with pleasure.

Illustrations: GERRY GERSTEN

Index

Index

Martinez, John, 175
55 Hudson Street
New York, NY 10013

Mattelson, Marvin, 138, 304
88 Lexington Avenue
New York, NY 10016

Mayer, Bill, 147, 323
240 Forkner Drive
Decatur, GA 30030

Mazzotta, Jim, 181
2350 Lafayette Street
Fort Myers, FL 33901

McCaffrey, Peter, 182
141 Second Avenue #16
New York, NY 10003

McCollum, Rick, 157
111 Saugatuck Avenue
Westport, CT 06880

McCollum, Sudi, 397, 417
10184 Parkwood Drive #5
Cupertino, CA 95014

McDonald, Jerry, 317
180 Clipper Street
San Francisco, CA 94114

McGinnis, Robert E., 7, 79, 202
13 Arcadia Road
Old Greenwich, CT 06870

McKinnon, Lyn D.S., 371
136 Brown Road
Howell, NJ 07731

McLean, Wilson, 244, 261, 352, 355,
    399, 411
902 Broadway
New York, NY 10010

McHamon, Mark M., 302, 427, 482
2620 Highland Avenue
Evanston, IL 60201

McMahon, Mary Burzynski, 295
666 Euclid Avenue South #815
Cleveland, OH 44114

McMullan, James, 58, 78, 211,
    376, 386
99 Lexington Avenue
New York, NY 10016

Meltzoff, Stanley, 90, 92, 93
128 Grange Avenue
Fair Haven, NJ 07701

Mendelson, Steve, 104
7216 Flower Street
Takoma Park, MD 20912

Mihaesco, Eugene, 64, 68, 116
140 Waverly Place
New York, NY 10014

Mikolaycak, Charles, 194
64 East 91 Street
New York, NY 10028

Minor, Wendell, 46, 100, 188,
    220, 235
277 West Fourth Street
New York, NY 10014

Mistretta, Andrea, 493
5 Bohnert Place
Waldwick, NJ 07463

Mitchell, Dick, 509
% Richards, Sullivan, Brock & Assoc.
12700 Hillcrest Road
Dallas, TX 75230

Montiel, David, 223
115 West 16 Street
New York, NY 10011

Morello, Robert, 410
205 St. John's Place
Brooklyn, NY 11217

Morris, Frank, 37, 122, 227
23 Bethune Street
New York, NY 10014

Nachreiner, Tom, 309
N6 W30662 Mohawk Trail
Waukesha, WI 53186

Neary, Scott, 36
81 St. Marks Place
New York, NY 10003

Nelson, Bill, 368, 435, 436, 505
1402 Wilmington Avenue
Richmond, VA 23227

Nemirov, Meredith, 391
110 Kent Street
Brooklyn, NY 11222

Nessim, Barbara, 23, 133
240 East 15 Street
New York, NY 10003

Notarile, Chris, 12
11 Hamilton Avenue
Cranford, NJ 07016

Odom, Mel, 132
252 West 76 Street
New York, NY 10023

Olbinski J. Rafal, 465
131 East Seventh Street
New York, NY 10003

Olson, Robert A., 446, 513
15215 Buchanan Court
Eden Prairie, MN 55344

Orlando, Paul, 508, 510
4202 Herbert Avenue
St. Louis, MO 63134

Otnes, Fred, 65, 276, 299, 396
Chalburn Road
West Redding, CT 06896

Ovies, Joseph, 453
1 Park Place #S120
1900 Emery Street NW
Atlanta, Ga 30318

Palencar, John Jude, 207
6763 Middlebrook Boulevard
Middleburg Heights, OH 44130

Palma, Philip, 452
Road 3 158 B
Blairstown, NJ 07825

Palulian, Dickran, 314, 516
18 McKinley Street
Rowayton, CT 06853

Panter, Gary, 137
2012 North Beachwood Drive
Hollywood, CA 90068

Pardue, Jack, 56
2307 Sherwood Hall Lane
Alexandria, VA 22306

Pascoe, Lea, 333
220 Newport Center Drive
Newport Beach, CA 92660

Pate, Martin, 523
1700 Golden Gate Drive NW
Atlanta, GA 30309

Peak, Bob, 382, 421, 524
% Harvey Kahn Associates, Inc.
50 East 50 Street
New York, NY 10022

Pearson, Doug, 500
% O'Grady Galleries
333 North Michigan
Chicago, IL 60601

Pedersen, Judy, 526
96 Greene Street
New York, NY 10012

Pepper, Bob, 490
157 Clinton Street
Brooklyn, NY 11201

Pertchik, Harriet, 468
21 Sinclair Martin Drive
Roslyn, NY 11576

Pinkney, Jerry, 239, 310, 331
41 Furnace Dock Road
Croton-On-Hudson, NY 10502

Provensen, Alice, 241
Clinton Hollow—Rural Delivery
Staatsburg, NY 12580

Provensen, Martin, 241
Clinton Hollow—Rural Delivery
Staatsburg, NY 12580

Pyle, Chuck, 361
146 Tenth Avenue
San Francisco, CA 94118

Reid, Charles, 143, 247, 272
81 Clapboard Hill Road
Green's Farms, CT 06436

Reynolds, Scott, 42, 146
308 West 30 Street
New York, NY 10001

Ribes, Fredericka, 230, 231
203 Seventh Avenue
Brooklyn, NY 11215

Richardson, Hiram, 205
10 Log Cabin Terrace
Sparta, NJ 07871

Rixford, Ellen, 294
308 West 97 Street, Apt. 71
New York, NY 10025

Robin, Leslie, 198
P.O. Box 127
Glencoe, IL 60022

Rodriguez, Robert, 193
618 South Western
Los Angeles, CA 90005

Romero, Javier, 206
231 West 26 Street
New York, NY 10001

Roth, Arnold, 191
P.O. Box 1219
Princeton, NJ 08540

Rovillo, Chris, 512
% Richards, Sullivan, Brock & Assoc.
12700 Hillcrest Road
Dallas, TX 75230

Ruddell, Gary, 63, 502
378 Belmont Street
Oakland, CA 94610

Rush, John, 179
123 Kedzie Street
Evanston, IL 60202

Sano, Kazuhiko, 224, 381, 491
729 B Waller Street
San Francisco, CA 94117

Santore, Charles, 357
138 South 20 Street
Philadelphia, PA 19103

Schlecht, Richard, 26
2724 South June Street
Arlington, VA 22202

Schmelzer, John P., 514, 522
539 North Thatcher Avenue
River Forest, IL 60305

Schottland, Miriam, 415
42 West 76 Street
New York, NY 10023

Schwab, Michael, 306
410 Townsend Street
San Francisco, CA 94107

Schwartz, Daniel, 27, 81, 256, 398
48 East 13 Street
New York, NY 10003

Scoggins, Timothy, 503
23930 Ocean Avenue #109
Torrance, CA 90505

Seaver, Jeff, 409, 470
130 West 24 Street
New York, NY 10011

Selby, Bill, 275
5203 Fenwat Court D
Columbus, OH 43214

Selby, Bob, 86
143 Glenwood Avenue
Pawtucket, RI 02860

Sharpe, Jim, 363
5 Side Hill Road
Westport, CT 06880

Shay, R.J., 74
343 Hillside Avenue
St. Louis, MO 63119

Sherr, Ronald, 35
159 Second Avenue
New York, NY 10003

Shilstone, Arthur, 32
42 Picketts Ridge Road
West Redding, CT 06896

Shurtleff, Gini, 18
84-09 155 Avenue
Lindenwood, NY 11414

Sienkiewicz, Bill, 408, 494
20 Lincoln Street
Westport, CT 06880

Silverman, Burt, 52, 97 99, 374
324 West 71 Street
New York, NY 10023

Singer, Alan, 416, 461
30 Hightop Lane
Jericho, NY 11753

Singer, Arthur, 416, 461
30 Hightop Lane
Jericho, NY 11753

Skolsky, Mark, 407
429 East 82 Street
New York, NY 10028

Slack, Chuck, 106
9 Cambridge Lane
Lincolnshire, IL 60015

Sloan, William A., 492
444 East 82 Street
New York, NY 10028

Smith, Douglas, 120, 136
405 Washington Street
Brookline, MA 02146

Smith, Elwood, 71, 121, 334
2 Locust Grove Road
Rhinebeck, NY 12572

Smith, Joseph A., 166
159 John Street
New York, NY 10038

Sorel, Edward, 72, 83, 117
156 Franklin Street
New York, NY 10013

Spanfeller, Jim, 170
Mustato Road
Katonah, NY 10536

Sparks, Richard, 148, 278, 438
2 West Rocks Road
Norwalk, CT 06851

Spitzmiller, Walt, 69, 70, 145
24 Lee Lane
West Redding, CT 06896

Index

ART DIRECTORS

CLIENTS

Index

ADVERTISING

64
REASONS TO ATTEND

The faculty:
Alan E. Cober,
Mark English,
Bernie Fuchs,
Bob Heindel,
Fred Otnes,
Robert Peak,
Seymour Chwast,
John deCesare,
Alan Peckolick.
Past guests include:
Lorraine Allen,
Sam Antupit,
Darwin Bahm,
Walter Bernard,
Roger Black,
Herb Bleiweiss,
Ahden Busch,
Jacquelin Casey,
Dick Coyne,
Kinuko Y. Craft,
Jacqueline Dedell,
Etienne Delessert,
Harry O. Diamond,
Leo and Diane Dillon,
Bill Erlacher,
Gordon Fisher,
Phyllis Flood,
Dick Gangel,
Fritz Gottschalk,
Rudy Hoglund,
Nigel Holmes,
Judeth Jampel,

THE ILLUSTRATORS
& DESIGNERS
WORKSHOP

The Workshop includes presentations by the
faculty and guests, visits to the studios
and offices of faculty members, one-to-one
portfolio reviews, demonstrations and crits
of a live assignment, issued to registrants
prior to the event.

Write for more detailed information to:
The Illustrators Workshop Inc.
P.O. Box 3447, Noroton, CT 06820 U.S.A.
(203) 655-8394

Harvey Kahn,
Herb Lubalin,
Robert L. Mayotte,
Rick McCollum,
Gerald McConnell,
Wilson McLean,
David Merrill,
Susan E. Meyer,
Duane Michals,
Eugene Mihaesco,
Lou Myers,
Barbara Nessim,
Jack O'Grady,
Howard Paine,
George Parker,
Al Parker,
Art Paul,
Martin Pedersen,
Margery Peters,
Jerry Pinkney,
Don Ivan Punchatz,
Walt Reed,
Jeffrey Schrier,
Leslie Segal,
Maurice Sendak,
Neil Shakery,
Lou Silverstein,
Elwood H. Smith,
Donald Smolen,
Ed Soyka,
Atha Tehon,
Jessica Weber,
Mary Zisk.

DENNIS LUZAK

POST OFFICE BOX 342 REDDING RIDGE, CONNECTICUT 06876 203·938·3158

Representative Joanne Palulian, #18 McKinley St., Rowayton, Connecticut 06853 203-866-3734

David Plourde

The Little Browne Book

pema browne ltd.
369-1925

185 east 85th st., new york, 10028

Illustration and Literary Agents
PERRY J. BROWNE
PEMA BROWNE

John Rush

Paul Reott

George Angelini

Ted Enik

Joe Burleson

Ron Jones

Glee LoScalzo

ILLUSTRATION

PAST

Howard Pyle

PRESENT

Bernie Fuchs

FUTURE

Richard Powers

We have a large stock of original illustrations available for collectors of almost every special interest, by name, subject, medium, style—and price range.

We also publish the ILLUSTRATION COLLECTORS NEWSLETTER to which you can subscribe for $7.50 a year. Or, send $2.00 for a sample copy.

Call us or come for a visit to our gallery—an hour from mid-Manhattan by car or train. For appointment, call Walt or Roger Reed at (203) 838-0486.

ILLUSTRATION HOUSE, INC.

53 Water Street South Norwalk, Connecticut 06854

PETER FIORE

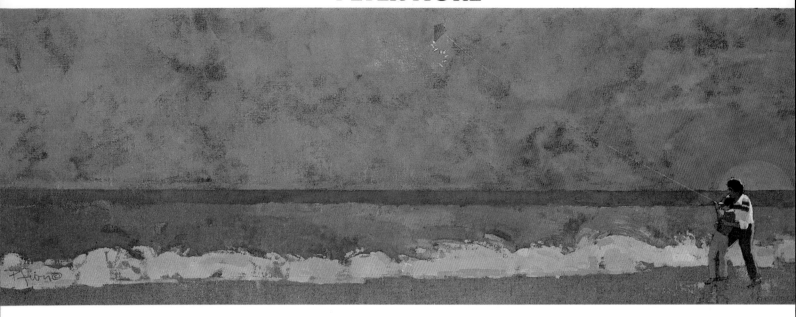

CHUCK HAMRICK

ROB SAUBER

JEFFREY TERRESON

CLIFF SPOHN

JIM CAMPBELL

PAUL TANKERSLEY

MICHAEL NOOMÉ

JOHN EGGERT

RUDY LASLO

GEOFFREY McCORMACK

JONATHAN MILNE

MICHAEL SMOLLIN

ANN MEISEL

DAN BROWN

MIKE MIKOS

CHRIS NOTARILE

DAVID SCHLEINKOFER

BOB JONES

RICHARD LEECH

TED MICHENER

JEFFREY MANGIAT

TOM NEWSOM

BEN WOHLBERG

CHUCK GILLIES

MITCHELL HOOKS

JOHN SOLIE

DENNIS LYALL

What do all these brushes have in common?

Through almost a century of making the finest quality artist paper, we have developed an attitude: Taking our time and doing it right. And giving our customers the finest quality products we know you demand and appreciate. We're proud to have developed a supply of Strathmore Brushes which artists tell us are worthy of the Strathmore quality.

Strathmore Brushes for Oil and Acrylic

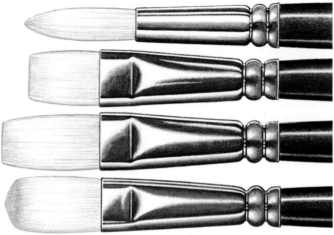

Strathmore Superior Quality Hog Bristle
The highest quality ChungKing Bristle. Designed with the natural curve of the hair to interlock, giving extra spring. Each hair has unique natural split to hold more color. The ultimate quality for oil and acrylic painting.

Strathmore Fine Quality Hog Bristle
Designed with interlocking formation with natural Hog Bristle. High quality silky hair always springs back to original fine shape.

Strathmore White
Top quality synthetic fiber retains good spring and sharp working edge.

Strathmore Red Sable
Excellent natural spring and sharp point. Ideal for fine work of oil and acrylic painting.

Strathmore Sabeline
The finest European Sabeline hair. Excellent performance with good spring and sharp point.

Strathmore Brushes for Watercolor

Strathmore Kolinsky
The finest Kolinsky hair. Extraordinary natural spring and fine point.

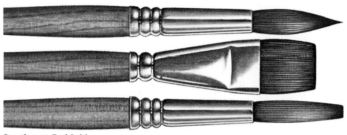

Strathmore Red Sable
The next best to our Kolinsky. Excellent spring and holds a good amount of color.

Strathmore Sabeline
The finest European Sabeline hair. Good spring and natural fine point. Inexpensive.

Strathmore Squirrel
Untrimmed French-dressed natural hair forms a needle-point tip. Inexpensive.

Strathmore White
The highest quality synthetic fiber. Clean, sharp working edge.

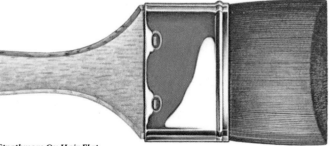

Strathmore Ox Hair Flat
The finest quality ox hair, beautifully shaped to retain sharp working edge. Excellent wash brush.

©1983 Strathmore Paper Co., Westfield, MA 01085

A Strathmore brush outperforms every other brush in its class.

JACK UNRUH
A distinctive style with a fresh new look

DOUG PIERSON
A fantastic new talent in airbrush realism

DAN FORD
A great new look with a dramatic flair for products

BART FORBES
A unique watercolor style with a worldwide following

JO SICKBERT
America's leading primitive artist

PAINTING BY DOUG PIERSON

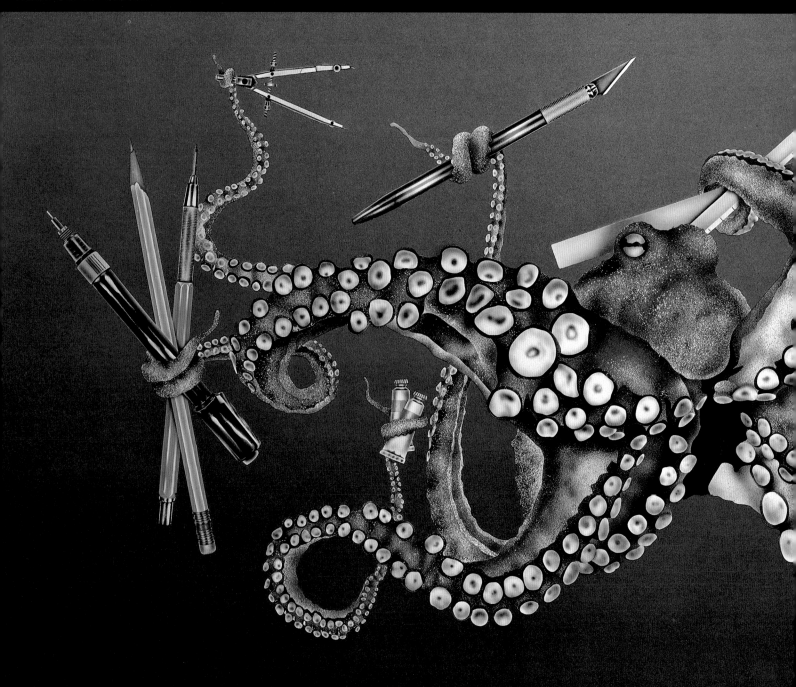

ADVERTISING ARTS

333 N. MICHIGAN
CHICAGO, IL 60601
312/726-9833

TONY WEITZ
The leading contemporary African artist

ROBERT GUNN
In the Rockwell tradition of American illustration

BILL PAPAS
International watercolorist and figure painter

BOB MEYER
A special combination of design and illustration

STEVE HENDRICKS
A fluid style that breathes life into illustration

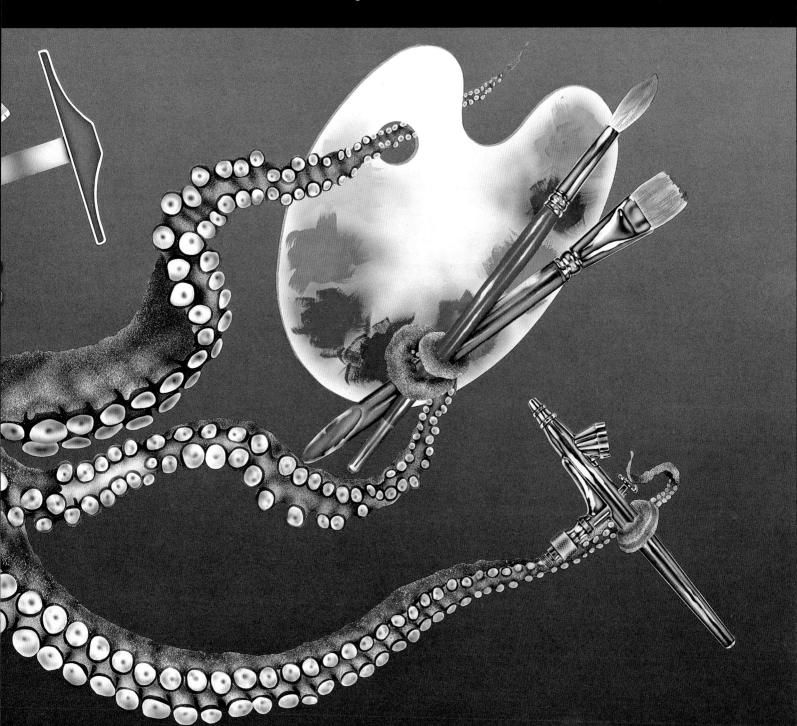

- Competitive costs
  - Flexibility in production time
    - Knowledge of sales reps
      - Service, Labor quality
        - Financial stability

Can you expect all of these from your printer ?

The Society of Illustrators has come to us since its annual book, "Illustrators 23."

Artists Representative

Bronson Potter & Rala Ashworth
pictures by Carol Nicklaus

KIRCHOFF/WOHLBERG, INC.

866 UNITED NATIONS PLAZA, NEW YORK, NY 10017   212-644-2020

897 BOSTON POST ROAD, MADISON, CT 06443   203-245-7308

OUR TEN COMMANDMENTS of ARTIST REPRESENTATION

1. We represent only artists we believe in and are totally committed to them.

2. We believe in being more than agents and become involved in the *total career* of the artists we represent.

3. We appreciate the problems of the artist and try, whenever possible, to alleviate these problems.

4. We also appreciate the problems of the art director: his client-agency relationship, tight deadlines and budget limitations and try to help him solve these problems whenever we can.

5. We believe in *full representation.* That means taking on only that number of artists that we can fully represent as well as insuring that each artist is non-competitive in style with other artists we represent.

6. We believe in giving *full service* to our artists and to the art director, promptly and professionally. Every client, no matter what the job price, deserves the very best we can offer.

7. We believe in being *flexible.* Business conditions change. The economy rises and falls. Accounts switch. We and our artists must adjust to all changes in order to successfully survive.

8. We believe in always meeting deadlines and always keeping a bargain. We and our artists are only as good as our word and our last job.

9. We believe in *BEING HONEST* at all times. With our artists. With the art director. With ourselves.

10. And finally, we believe in our *profession...* the profession of representing artists. We firmly believe that it is the most exciting and challenging profession anywhere and we are proud to be a part of it.

**Barbara Gordon
Associates Ltd.
165 East 32 Street
New York, N.Y. 10016
212-686-3514**

RAYMOND KURSÁR

To view the Artists' Portfolio,
or to arrange for a Slide Presentation, Call or write to:
Raymond Kursár ~ One Lincoln Plaza ~ New York, N.Y. 10023
(212) 873~5605

REINGOLD

It Takes Masters To Make Masters . . .

RAPIDOGRAPH®

...pen-and-ink textures by Dan Puffer

It is obvious that Dan Puffer, a metallurgical engineer by profession, has mastered the challenge of his avocation—Rapidograph pen-and-ink drawing. He interprets dramatically the textures of objects in his environment, such as the pitted coral blocks of an unfinished, long-abandoned cathedral on Bermuda, of weathered and saw-marked shingles, of tree bark and grassy fields, of a butterfly and peeling paint.

While the artist's skills are the essential ingredient for this demanding task, the hours of dependable output provided by his Rapidograph pens are equally impressive. Tubular nib (available in 13 line widths) allows the Rapidograph pen to move in any direction on virtually any drawing surface (including acetate and glass) with the ease of, and with even less pressure than pencil, making it far more versatile and less fatiguing to use than crow quill or wing-nib pens. Refillable ink cartridge is another artist-pleasing feature, permitting long, uninterrupted drawing sessions at home or in the field or studio.

The patented DRY DOUBLE-SEAL™ cap keeps ink throughout the

These drawings by Dan Puffer are copyrighted by the artist and may not be reproduced for any reason without written permission from the artist. Original drawings range from 8″ x 11″ to 14″ x 20″.

ART

balanced ink-flow system fluid, ready for instant startup and optimum drawing time. No maintenance-plagued gimmicks for sealing or humidifying. Accept no substitutes. Look for the *Koh-I-Noor Rapidograph* on the pen holder to be sure you have the most widely accepted and proven technical pen in the United States and Canada.

"Get-acquainted" packaging (Product No. 3165-BX) offers a special saving with pen/ink combination and your choice of the five most popular Rapidograph line widths. Single pens and pen sets in a number of configurations are also available. Ask your dealer or send the coupon for details: Koh-I-Noor Rapidograph, Inc., Bloomsbury, NJ 08804 (201) 479-4124. In Canada: 1815 Meyerside Dr., Mississauga, Ont. L5T 1B4 (416) 671-0696.

KOH-I-NOOR
RAPIDOGRAPH®

Koh-I-Noor Rapidograph,Inc., 100 North St., Bloomsbury, NJ 08804 (201) 479-4124
In Canada: 1815 Meyerside Drive, Mississauga, Ont. L5T 1B4 (416) 671-0696

©1983 Koh-I-Noor Rapidograph, Inc. All rights reserved.
®RAPIDOGRAPH is a Registered Trademark of Koh-I-Noor Rapidograph, Inc.

Please send complimentary Catalog "E" describing Rapidograph technical pens. Koh-I-Noor and Pelikan inks and other artist materials.
☐ Please send me names of Koh-I-Noor dealers in my area.

Name (please print or type)

Company Name if the following is a business address

Number and Street, RD and Box, etc.

City _____ State _____ Zip _____

Koh-I-Noor Rapidograph, Inc., 100 North St., Bloomsbury, NJ 08804
In Canada: 1815 Meyerside Dr. Mississauga, Ont. L5T 1B4

Alan E. Cohen

B. Fuchs.

Gerstu

NICHOLAS GAETANO

WILSON McLEAN:

B. Peak

Isadore Seltzer

**Harvey Kahn
Associates, Inc.**

*50 East 50th St. New York, NY 10022
212 752-8490*

Doug Kahn, Associate

GREG HILDEBRANDT
Represented by:
UNICORN
90 Park Avenue
Verona, NJ 07044
(201) 239-7088

Greg Hildebrandt —
artist/illustrator — "My
professional interests
center around using and
further developing my
ability to convey, through
visual media, thoughts,
ideas and concepts."

Representative clients:
Omni Magazine
Bantam Books
Ballantine Books
Random House
Golden Books
Simon & Schuster
Warner Brothers Records
MGM
Verkerke Reproductions
Columbia Pictures
Roach Incorporated
William Morrow
3M Corporation
20th Century Fox
Lucas Films
Platt & Munk
Western Publishing
Holt, Rinehart & Winston
The Bill Gold Agency
Young & Rubicam
Dellafemina Travisano
Warner Communications
ABC
Creamer Inc.
Goldmann Verlag
Starlog
Heavy Metal
American Publishing
Pacific Comics
Warren Paper

immortals

barnett plotkin · 230 east 44 st · n.y., n.y. 10017 · (212) 661 · 7149

BILL ERLACHER ARTISTS ASSOCIATES

ARTISTS REPRESENTED

NORMAN ADAMS

DON BRAUTIGAM

MICHAEL DEAS

MARK ENGLISH

ALEX GNIDZIEJKO

ROBERT HEINDEL

STEVE KARCHIN

DICK KREPEL

SKIP LIEPKE

RICK McCOLLUM

FRED OTNES

DANIEL SCHWARTZ

211 EAST 51 STREET, NEW YORK, NEW YORK 10022 (212) 755-1365/6 ASSOCIATE: NICOLE EDELL

FRED OTNES

"Each of Otnes' collages incorpo-
rates a remarkable range and depth
of knowledge—not only the technical know-how that flows from his
fingertips, not only the traditional
training that he absorbed at the
Art Institute and the American
Academy of Art in Chicago, not
only the modern photographic-
printing-lithographic technology
that he has mastered, not only the
influences of other present-day
painters that he has adapted to his
own vision, but also the supple-
mentary acquisition of a staggering
amount of information about the
special subject he is illustrating and
illuminating."

—Jim Hoffman,
Graphis Magazine, No. 188

Represented by Bill Erlacher, Artists Associates, 211 East 51 Street, New York, NY 10019, 212-755-1365/6

R. Heindel

S T E V E • K A R C H I N

©1984

B O X E S • C O L L A G E S

MARK ENGLISH

"BEACH SCENE"

12" X 16" OIL ON CANVAS

SKIP LIEPKE

BILL ERLACHER ARTISTS ASSOCIATES 211 EAST 51 STREET NEW YORK NEW YORK 10022 (212) 755-1365/6

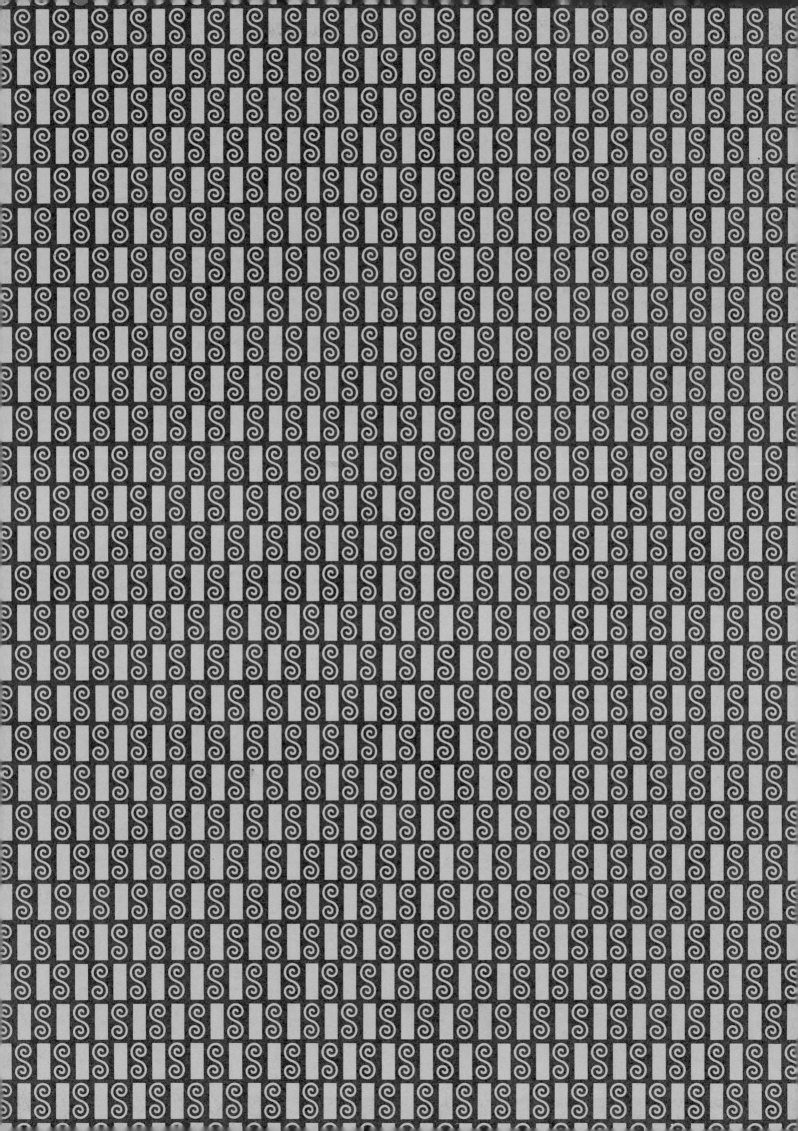